EXPOSING THE K-12 HIDDEN CURRICULUM ON DIVERSITY

A Photographic Approach

JAMES H. BANNING, PH.D.

TerraCotta Publishing

EXPOSING THE K-12 HIDDEN CURRICULUM ON DIVERSITY

James H. Banning© 2019

Email: campusecologist@gmail.com

Website: http://www.campusecologist.com

ISBN 13: 978-0-9983168-1-9

ISBN 10: 0-9983168-1-4

Library of Congress Control Number:2019910624

Cover design and typesetting by Michelle Kenny, Windsor, CO

Printed in the United States of America

TerraCotta Publishing

Arvada, CO

TerraCotta
Publishing

A companion book to

Campus Artifacts as Diversity Messages:
A Photographic Approach (2018)

TABLE OF CONTENTS

An Introductory Note _____ *xi*

Preface _____ *xii*

Acknowledgments _____ *xvii*

Chapter One: Introduction and the Hidden Curriculum _____ 1

Introduction: The Hidden Curriculum _____ 2

Definitional Characteristics of the Hidden Curriculum ___ 2

Hidden Curriculum: Important Questions _____ 3

The Hidden Curriculum: The Material Culture
and Diversity Messages _____ 4

References _____ 6

Bibliography for the Hidden Curriculum _____ 9

**Chapter Two: The Hidden Curriculum: Visual/Photographic
Tools to Interpret the K-12 Schools' Visual Material Culture** _ 23

Non-Verbal Communications and the Hidden
Curriculum _____ 22

The Interpretation of Photographs _____ 27

Tools for Interpretation of Photographs: An Eclectic
Approach _____ 28

Summary _____ 32

References _____ 33

Chapter Three: Photographing K-12 School Diversity Messages _____ 35

What I Bring to the Interpretative Process _____ 35

Using the Eclectic Interpretative Frame for Understanding Diversity Messages _____ 40

Basic Question: Are the Diversity Messages Manifest or Latent? _____ 40

Additional Questions: Tools for Deconstruction _____ 41

Moving from Individual Photos to Cultural Themes _____ 46

A Taxonomy for K-12 Hidden Curriculum Artifacts Illustrations _____ 51

Summary_____ 57

References _____ 58

Chapter Four: Collection and Utilization of Diversity Photographs _____ 61

Strategies for Collection and Participation _____ 61

Ethical Issue: Photographing School Artifacts _____ 68

Summary _____ 69

References _____ 70

Appendix A: *Campus Artifacts as Diversity Messages: A Photographic Approach*_____ 73

(Chapter One: Lines of Scholarship: The Ecological Perspective, Material Culture, and Visual/Photographic Observations.)

Appendix B: Material Culture, Behavior, and the Physical Trace Approach to Assessment _____ 91

About the Author _____103

Shade Boxes

Shade Box 2-1: Illustration of Rapport's Mnemonic Function _____ 24

Shade Box 3-1: My Interpretative Stance on Diversity ___ 35

Shade Box 4-1: Removal of School Artifacts _____ 63

Shade Box 4-2: Bumper Sticker Ethnography _____ 65

Shade Box Appendix A-1: Resource References for the Ecological Perspective _____ 76

Shade Box Appendix A-2: Resource References for Material Culture _____ 78

Shade Box Appendix A-3: Resource References for Visual/ Photographic Research_____ 82

AN INTRODUCTORY NOTE

In 1984, J. B. Jackson, a pioneer landscape scholar, noted the following:

> Over and over again. I have said that the commonplace aspects of the contemporary landscape, the streets and houses and fields and places of work, could teach us a great deal not only about American history and American Society, but about ourselves and how we relate to the world. It is a matter of learning how to see.

The purpose of this book reflects J. B. Jackson's statement: "learning how to see" the halls and classrooms of K-12 schools and discovering the hidden messages focusing on diversity. Again, to use and transport Jackson's words: The school "is always open before us. We have but to read it."

Jackson quotes from: Mendelsohn, J. & Wilson, C. (Eds.). (2015). *Drawn to Landscape.* Staunton, VA: George F. Thompson Publishing.

PREFACE

The title of this book, *Exposing the K-12 Hidden Curriculum on Diversity: A Photographic Approach,* sums up the intent of the book: A practical illustration of how many of the diversity messages in our schools and classrooms are hidden in school artifacts, particularly posters and artworks, and how these messages can be captured by photography to promote discussion to improve the school experience for all. There is a materiality to school artifacts, but they interface with students, teachers, and other constituents in interpretative ways to produce multiple meanings, both its positive and negative aspects.

The material culture of the K-12 school comprises the human-made objects that are viewable by the inhabitants of the school, including those who spend a substantial amount of time—students, faculty, and staff—and the parent or visitor who spends a shorter time. Many of these objects are intentional and reflect considerable effort in design and implementation: the school buildings, institutional artifacts, furniture arrangements, official signage, and the installation of various classroom and hallway art forms—posters, paintings, murals, and sculptures. Often, however, the material culture on display is not officially intended, designed, or approved, and yet these items also send messages of culture, including messages of diversity, for example, graffiti, physical traces of behavior, and unofficial signage. In addition, even the objects intentionally designed for a specific message often take on meanings that were unintended.

The practical purpose of this book is to present a concise overview of ways 1) to view the K-12 artifacts in order to expose the hidden messages of diversity (conceptual tools), 2) to interpret and understand the diversity messages embedded in the artifacts (interpretative tools), and 3) ways to use photographs to expose the diversity messages for discussion. The basic conceptual tools involve the concepts of the ecological perspective, material culture, and visual/photographic research (Appendix A). These concepts provide the foundation for Chapter One's introduction of the important and organizing concept of the hidden curriculum and the use of photographs to expose its messages regarding diversity.

Chapter Two presents interpretive tools that are derived from the observational methods associated with environmental psychology and include an eclectic range of interpretative strategies primarily based on qualitative visual analysis.

In Chapter Three, after presenting the importance and complexity of interpretative strategies and photographic illustrations of diversity messages, a taxonomy/matrix is presented to assist in moving from individual photographs to school themes. Photographs are presented to illustrate the use of the matrix and to highlight the often-found hidden messages in the classroom and school culture regarding students of color, female students, LGBTQ students, and differently-abled students.

Chapter Four presents a discussion of ways to collect and utilize photographs of diversity in the hidden curriculum. Individual and group strategies are presented, highlighting the importance of participation and feedback as a way for a school to move toward a more inclusive and positive learning environment for all students. A brief discussion is also presented on the removal of school artifacts. The chapter closes with a discussion of ethical considerations important to photographing the hidden curriculum of the school.

In summary, this book takes the position that for a school culture to be positive and healthy, all students need to feel welcomed and not ignored, safe and not endangered, and included rather than excluded. Given the changing nature of schools and the importance of social justice, the hidden curriculum diversity messages associated with race, ethnicity, physical abilities, gender, sexual identities, and religion are ones that require teacher and school staff attention.

A final note: Apologies to the reader and to "real" photographers for the quality of many of the photographs. They were taken during field activities where the focus was on capturing content for discussions.

ACKNOWLEDGMENTS

I would like to thank all the K-12 schools and teachers that have invited me to read, interpret, and discuss their school environments. These are not always easy discussions, and I appreciate their sincere engagement. These schools and teachers will not be named nor will photographs be associated with specific schools. The photographs are very helpful in illustrating issues and giving practical examples for the concepts and tools of the book, but they represent only a "slice in time" for schools and their classrooms.

Many of the negative and troublesome photos have been addressed by the schools; therefore, the photographs should be associated with the purpose of understanding the concepts and tools of the book and should not serve to embarrass a school or teacher.

I would also like to thank Sue Banning, who as always, has given both personal and conceptual support to this project: always available to discuss ideas, edit my words, correct my spelling, provide constructive feedback, and give me the personal encouragement every writer needs.

In addition, there are many colleagues who have been persons of influence.

On the topic of photographing school diversity, I would like to acknowledge Val Middleton, Terri Dennison, Ellyn Dickmann, Shelby Maier, Stephanie Cox, and the legacy of Sharon Bartels (1937 –1998).

Thanks to Dr. Andrea Sims and TerraCotta Publishing for placing my thoughts in book form.

1

INTRODUCTION AND THE
HIDDEN CURRICULUM

"The hidden curriculum consists of those things pupils learn through the experience of attending school rather than the stated educational objectives . . ." (Harakambos & Holborn, 1990, Sociology, p. 242).

The purpose of this book is to provide very practical ways to read and interpret the material culture of the K-12 classrooms and hallways focusing on diversity messages. It is unwise to be practical, however, without at least noting some background scholarship for the practical efforts. Practice without theory is risky. The presentation of related scholarship will be in two formats. First, the background scholarship for understanding the importance of the ecological perspective (environments influence behavior), material culture (what we put on the walls contain messages that can influence behavior) and visual/photographic research (using photographs of the material culture to capture the messages for discussion) is presented in Appendix A. Appendix A contains Chapter One, "Lines of Scholarship: The Ecological Perspective, Material Culture, and Visual/Photographic Observations," from the recent publication *Campus Artifacts as Diversity Messages*. This 2018 publication is similar in purpose to this manuscript, but with the site of interest being the college campus rather than the K-12 school environment. The second presentation of background scholarship for this manuscript is the presentation of a concept that has a long and extensive history with the K-12 school environment—the "hidden curriculum."

Introduction: The Hidden Curriculum

The task of introducing the concept of the hidden curriculum is not easy due to the enormous amount of scholarship associated with the concept and the numerous definitions associated with the concept. The notion of the hidden curriculum was introduced in 1968 (Jackson, 1968), but as of today you will find over 900,000 hits on Google and 67,000 hits on Google Scholar for "hidden curriculum." In addition, the ProQuest Dissertation & Theses Global™ database reports 378 doctoral dissertations using the concept in the title or abstract. Coupled with the enormity of background material, there are many definitions associated with the concept. My strategy for the introduction is to provide a comprehensive bibliography at the end of this chapter for those who would like to go into more depth/detail regarding the hidden curriculum concept. Also presented in this chapter is the relevant scholarship to support the purpose of this manuscript—illustrating that the messages of the material culture of K-12 classrooms and hallways are significant components of the school's hidden curriculum regarding diversity.

Definitional Characteristics of the Hidden Curriculum

The hidden curriculum of a school is what the school, generally unknowingly, teaches external to the formal curriculum. The formal curriculum is not hidden. It is the final public product produced by discussion and approval of entities related to school governance. Included in the formal curriculum is the approved content and often even details related to strategies to bring about student learning of the content. The hidden curriculum also has lessons to be learned, but the lessons are not often known or intended. The "hiddenness" of the lessons has been referred to as the unwritten, unofficial, and unintended (Abbott, 2014); unspoken (Adamson, 2013); implicit (Armstrong, Henson, & Savage); informal and inadvertent (Backhus, 2002); unstated (Brown & Kysilka, 2002); secret education (Bigelow, 1999); unwritten, latent, tacit, unstudied (Dreeben, 1976); unplanned (Henson, 2006); dark side (Jackson, 1992); deep level (Kidd, 1995,); shadowy, ill-defined, and amorphous (Sambell, & McDowell); and covert (McNeil, 1990). Schools have curriculums with hidden lessons. What are the important questions about these lessons?

The Hidden Curriculum: Important Questions

Given the vast scholarship associated with the concept of the hidden curriculum, only a small portion can be reported in this small manuscript focused on material culture and diversity messages. In addition to the foregoing introduction to definitions, there are several important questions that can be briefly addressed.

What gets hidden and where?

Haralambos (1990) suggests that the hidden curriculum of a school consists of what students learn through the experience of attending the school rather than the formal curriculum of the school. This learning is "transmitted though the everyday, normal goings-on in the schools" (McCutcheon, 1988 p. 191). These unintended learnings while attending school can be placed in categories. For example, Hemmings (2000) notes two categories within a school's hidden curriculum: structural and cultural. Structural hidden curriculum includes such items as class scheduling, nature of facilities, services, and unwritten school practices. The category of cultural hidden curriculum includes school rules and norms, relationships among groups, celebrations, and the material culture of the school (posters, artwork, graffiti, signs, murals, etc.). Giroux (1978) included as structural properties the school practices of "homogenous groupings, imposition of a common set of undifferentiated tasks; sharp polarization of power between the teacher and the students; and a reward-and-punishment system of evaluation" (p. 148). Jachim (1987) also offers similar levels to describe the hidden curriculum, structure, and content (p. 84). The structural component is similar to Hemmings, but Jachim also suggests structural components that are more physical in nature, for example, "seating arrangements, location of teacher's desk ..." (p. 84). The content category suggested by Jachim includes the symbolic messages received by the students from the hidden curriculum. The symbolic messages are cultural messages regarding a variety of issues including gender, race and ethnicity, sexual orientation, religious preferences, class, etc.

Who hides it? Intentionally or not?

Sockett (1992) suggests that the hidden curriculum could be concealed by someone or by an entity with "pernicious intent" related to some form of "conspiracy theory" (1992, p. 561). It could also be hidden just as an "unintended by-product" (Martin, 1983, p. 131). Meighan and Harber (2007) indicate that the notion of hidden has many ambiguities. They raise several possibilities: "Is it hidden intentionally to manipulate and persuade?" or "Is it hidden because no one notices or recognizes it?" or "Is it hidden because it has been forgotten or neglected?" or "Is it hidden because the originator has left?" (p. 80). This author takes the position that the hidden curriculum is hidden, not out of pernicious intent, but rather that elements of the hidden curriculum so accurately reflect the larger culture they go unnoticed, and are therefore hidden. Hannay (1984) promotes this idea by viewing the hidden curriculum as a vehicle for cultural reproduction. The similarity between the hidden curriculum and the voice of culture is captured by Porterfield (2013) in the use of the phrase "hidden in plain sight." This underscores that the hidden curriculum functions as a primary socialization process to reproduce and transmit the values of society including views on gender, sexual orientation, race, class, and other identity structures. For the purposes of this manuscript, Meighan and Harber's (2007) conclusion is adopted: "The outcomes of 'hidden' may be more significant than the reasons" (p. 78–79). This position leads us to the next section, where the outcomes of the hidden curriculum for students of diversity are discussed.

The Hidden Curriculum: The Material Culture and Diversity Messages

As noted earlier, the purpose of this manuscript is to explore hidden messages regarding diversity that are embedded in the visual material culture of school classrooms and hallways. The visual material includes posters, signage, murals, and other artwork. Looking at the hidden message being taught by visual culture of K-12 schools regarding diversity is not without supportive scholarship. For example, Adamson (2013), in the exploration of textbooks, noted that textbooks in all subject content have been criticized for the hidden curriculum that subtly teaches messages that celebrate some cultural groups while ignoring the efforts and contributions of other cultural, racial, and ethnic groups particularly in the use of illustrations. Andres (2006) notes the less-celebrated groups within the schools are most often "students, faculty, and staff who also happen to be women, people of color, from low socioeconomic status (SES) backgrounds, or those for whom English is an additional language" (p. 249). Unfortunately, members of these oppressed groups often internalize these negative messages in the hidden curriculum (Brown & Kysilka, 2002). Posters, signage, murals, sculpture, and other artwork in K-12 settings function like illustrations in textbooks. These elements of the school environment make up the "hidden visual curriculum" (Baker, Ng-He, & Lopez-Bush, 2008, p. 290). The content of the images of the material visual culture can send messages regarding identity, inclusion, roles in school and society, and many other cultural expectations. Cohen (1970, 1971, & 1975) supports the position that the processes of student socialization and enculturation are symbolically reinforced by school classroom decorations and artifacts, (i.e., the material culture of the school).

In this brief introduction, the interest in and importance of the hidden curriculum has been presented. Its definitional characteristics and the processes regarding its transmission have been established to support the aim of this manuscript—to explore the visual material culture of the hidden curriculum and the embedded messages regarding diversity. Chapter Two provides the visual/photographic tools to expose the embedded messages in school posters, signage, murals, etc. Chapter Three presents the application of these tools to school material culture and photographic illustrations of the findings. Chapter Four starts a discussion to answer the question of how to proceed to find the hidden curriculum and what to do if found.

References

Abbott, S. (2014). Hidden curriculum. In S. Abbott (Ed.). *The glossary of educational reform*. Retrieved from http://edglossary. org/hidden-curriclum.

Adamson, S. R. (2013*). Subtle messages: An examination of diversity in the illustrations of secondary level one French textbooks (*Doctoral Dissertation). Retrieved from the ProQuest Dissertation and Theses Global Database. (UMI No. 3557856)

Andres, E. (2006). The hidden curriculum in higher education: A book review. *Journal of Curriculum Studies, 38*(2), 246-249.

Armstrong, D. G., Henson, K. T. & Savage, T. V. (2001). *Teaching today: An introduction to education. 6th Edition.* Upper Saddle River, N.J.: Merrill Prentice Hall.

Backhus, D. A. (2002). It's not just a theory. Why Teachers need to address the nature of science and the "hidden curriculum. *The Science Teacher, 69*(4), 44-47.

Baker, M. H., Ng-He, C., & Lopez-Bosch, M.A. (2008). Reflections on the role of artist: A case study on the hidden curriculum of the Art Institute of Chicago. *Teaching Artist Journal, 6*(4), 290-297.

Brown, S. C. & Kysilka, M. L. (2002). *Applying multicultural and global concepts in the classroom and beyond.* Boston: Allyn & Bacon.

Bigelow, W. (1999). Probing the invisible life of schools. In C. Edelsky (Ed.). *Making justice our project: Teachers working toward critical whole language practices.* (242-257). Urbana,IL: National Council of Teachers of English.

Cohen, Y. (1970). Schools and civilization states. In J. Fischer, (Ed). *The social sciences and the comparative study of educational systems.* (pp. 55-147). Scranton, PA: International Textbook Company.

Cohen, Y. (1971). The shaping of men's mind: Adaptation to imperatives of Culture. In M. Wax, S. Diamond, & F. Gearing (Eds). *Anthropological perspective on Education.* (pp. 19-50). New York: Basic Books.

Cohen, Y. (1975). The state system, schooling, and cognitive and motivational patterns. In N. K Shimahara & A. Scrupski, (Eds.). *In Social forces and schooling: An anthropological and Sociological perspective.* (pp. 103-140). New York: David McKay.

Dreeben, R. (1976). The unwritten curriculum and its relation to values. *Journal of Curriculum Studies, 8*(2), 111-24.

Giroux, H. A. (1978). Developing educational programs: Overcoming the hidden curriculum. *The Clearing House, 52*(4), 148-151.

Hannay, L. M. (1984). *Cultural reproduction via the hidden curriculum (socialization, instruction)* (Doctoral Dissertation). Retrieved from the ProQuest Dissertation and Theses Global Database. (UMI No. 3287936)

Haralambos, M. & Holborn, M. (1990). *Sociology: Themes and perspectives.* London: Unwin Hyman.

Hemmings, A. (2000). The hidden curriculum corridor. *High School Journal, 83*(2), 1-10.

Henson, K. T. (1995). *Curriculum development for educational reform.* New York: HarperCollins.

Jachim. N. (1987). The hidden curriculum. *A Review of General Semantics, 44*(1), 83-85.

Jackson, P. W. (1968). *Life in classrooms.* New York: Holt, Rinehart and Winston, Inc.

Jackson, P. W. (1992). Conceptions of curriculum and curriculum specialists. In L. E. Beyer, & M.W. Apple (Eds). The curriculum:

Problems, politics, and possibilities. (3-40). Albany, NY: State University of New York Press.

Kidd, R. J. M. (1995). *Becoming a woman: Self, world and identity of primary school girls.*(Doctoral Dissertation). Retrieved from the ProQuest Dissertation and Theses Global Database. (UMI No. U077316)

Martin, J. (1983). What should we do we a hidden curriculum when we find one? In H. Giroux & D. Purpel. (Eds.). *The hidden curriculum and moral education.* (122-139). Berkeley, CA: McCutchan Publishing Corporation

Meighan, R. & Harber, C. (2007). *A sociology of educating.* 5th Ed. New York: Continuum.

McCutcheon, G. (1988). Curriculum and the work of teachers. In L. E. Beyer, & M. W. Apple (Eds). *The curriculum: Problems, politics, and possibilities.* (191-203). Albany, NY: State University of New York Press.

McNeil, J. D. (1990). *Curriculum: A comprehensive introduction*: New York: HarperCollins.

Porterfield, L. (2013). *Hidden in plain sight: Young Black women, place, and visual culture.* (Doctoral Dissertation). Retrieved from the ProQuest Dissertation and Theses Global Database. (UMI No. 3564850)

Sambell, K., & McDowell, L. (1998). The construction of the hidden curriculum: Messages and meanings in the assessment of student learning. *Assessment and Evaluation in Higher Education,23*(4), 591-402.

Sockett, H. (1992). The moral aspect of the curriculum. In P. W. Jackson, (Ed.). *Handbook of research on curriculum.* (543-569). New York: Macmillan Publishing Company.

Bibliography for Hidden Curriculum

Abbott, S. (2014). Hidden curriculum. In S. Abbott (Ed.). *The glossary of educational reform.* Retrieved from http://edglossary. org/hidden-curriclum.

Adamson, S. R. (2013*). Subtle messages: An examination of diversity in the illustrations of secondary level one French textbooks (*Doctoral Dissertation). Retrieved from the ProQuest Dissertation and Theses Global Database. (UMI No. 3557856)

Alsubaie, M. F. (2015). Hidden curriculum as one of current issues of curriculum. *Journal of Education and Practice.* 6(33), 125-128.

Andres, L. (2006). The hidden curriculum in higher education: A book review. *Journal of Curriculum Studies, 38*(2), 246-249.

Anyon, J. (1983). Social class and the hidden curriculum of work. In H. Giroux & D. Purpel. (Eds.). *The hidden curriculum and moral education.* (143-167). Berkeley, CA: McCutchan Publishing Corporation.

Apple, M. (1979). *Ideology and curriculum.* Boston: Routledge & Kegan.

Apple, M. & King, N. (1983). What do schools teach? In H. Giroux & D. Purpel. (Eds.). The hidden curriculum and moral education. (82-99). Berkeley, CA: McCutchan Publishing Corporation.

Apple, M. W. & Beyer, L. E. (1988). Social evaluation of curriculum. In L. E. Beyer, & M. W. Apple (Eds). *The curriculum: Problems, politics, and possibilities.* (334-350). Albany, NY: State University of New York Press.

Armstrong, D. G., Henson, K. T. & Savage, T. V. (2001). *Teaching today: An introduction to education. 6th Edition.* Upper Saddle River, N.J.: Merrill Prentice Hall.

Bailey, M. (2013). *Race, Class, Region and Gender in Early Emory School of Medicine Yearbooks* (Doctoral Dissertation). Retrieved from the ProQuest Dissertation and Theses Global Database. (UMI No. 3603924)

Baker, M. H., Ng-He, C., & Lopez-Bosch, M. A. (2008). Reflections on the role of artist: A case study on the hidden curriculum of the school of the Art Institute of Chicago. *Teaching Artist Journal, 6*(4), 290-297.

Backhus, D. A. (2002). It's not just a theory. Why Teachers need to address the nature of science and the "hidden curriculum. *The Science Teacher, 69*(4), 44-47.

Baldwin-Brown, A. (2017). *Exploratory examination of teaching the hidden curriculum in a classroom program to children with autism spectrum disorder.* (Doctoral Dissertation). Retrieved from the ProQuest Dissertation and Theses Global Database. (UMI No. 10686127)

Bible, D. E. (2013). *Out of the Academic closet: Heteronormativity, hidden curriculum, and the experience of lesbian and gay students in higher education* (Doctoral Dissertation). Retrieved from the ProQuest Dissertation and Theses Global Database. (UMI No. 3575120)

Bigelow, W. (1990). Inside the classroom: Social vision and critical pedagogy. *Teachers College Record, 91*(3), 437-448.

Bigelow, W. (1999). Probing the invisible life of schools. In C. Edelsky (Ed.), *Making justice our project: Teachers working toward critical whole language practices.* (242-257). Urbana, IL: National Council of Teachers of English.

Bigelow, W. (2004). The hidden curriculum: Helping students reflect critically on issues of schools, equity, and justice. In J. L. Kacheloe & D. Weil (eds.). *Critical thinking & Learning: An encyclopedia for parents & teachers.* (135-144). Westport, CT: Greenwood Press.

Brown, S. C. & Kysilka, M. L. (2002). *Applying multicultural and global concepts in the classroom and beyond.* Boston: Allyn & Bacon.

Burke, P. A. Y. (1983). *A study to determine the trends in attitude toward science among fourth, fifth and sixth grade male and female students* (Doctoral Dissertation). Retrieved from the ProQuest Dissertation and Theses Global Database. (UMI No. 3575120)

Cagan, E. (1978). Individualism, collectivism, and radical educational reform. *Harvard Educational Review, 48*(2), 227-266

Carl, N. M. (2017). A hidden curriculum of control: The inequities of urban schooling. (Doctoral Dissertation). Retrieved from the ProQuest Dissertation and Theses Global Database. (UMI No. 10278583)

Carpenter, V. M. & Lee, D. (2010). Teacher education and the hidden curriculum of heteronormality. *Curriculum Matter, 6*, 99-119.

Carvallo, O. R. (1995). *Vales in the hidden curriculum: An axiological reproduction* (Doctoral Dissertation). Retrieved from the ProQuest Dissertation and Theses Global Database. (UMI No. 9533941)

Champie, J. (1984). Is total communication enough? The hidden curriculum. *American Annuals of the Deaf, 129*(3), 347-318.

Cohen, Y. (1970). Schools and civilization states. In J. Fischer, (Ed). *The social sciences and the comparative study of educational systems.* (pp. 55-147). Scranton, PA: International Textbook Company.

Cohen, Y. (1971). The shaping of men's mind: Adaptation to imperatives of Culture. In M. Wax, S. Diamond, & F. Gearing (Eds). *Anthropological perspective on Education.* (pp. 19-50). New York: Basic Books.

Cohen, Y. (1975). The state system, schooling, and cognitive and motivational patterns. In N. K Shimahara & A. Scrupski, (Eds.).

In *Social forces and schooling: An anthropological and Sociological perspective.* (pp. 103-140). New York: David McKay.

Cornbleth, C. (1984). Beyond hidden curriculum. *Journal of Curriculum Studies 16*(1), 29-36.

Corrales, N. (1998). *The hidden curriculum of gender in elementary Spanish textbooks.* (Doctoral Dissertation). Retrieved from the ProQuest Dissertation and Theses Global Database. (UMI No. 9906895)

Dreeben, R. (1976). The unwritten curriculum and its relation to values. *Journal of Curriculum Studies, 8*(2), 111-24.

Eisner, E. (1992). Curriculum ideologies. In L. E. Beyer, & M.W. Apple (Eds). *The curriculum: Problems, politics, and possibilities.* (302-326). Albany, NY: State University of New York Press.

Elmore, R. & Sykes, G. (1992). Curriculum policy. In L. E. Beyer, & M.W. Apple (Eds). *The curriculum: Problems, politics, and possibilities.* (185-215). Albany, NY: State University of New York Press.

Erickson, F. & Shultz, J. (1992). Student's experience of the curriculum. In P. W. Jackson (Ed.). *Handbook of research on curriculum* (465-485). New York: MacMillan Publishing Co.

Erickson, S. K. (2007). *Engineering the hidden curriculum: How women doctoral students in engineering navigate belonging* (Doctoral Dissertation). Retrieved from the ProQuest Dissertation and Theses Global Database. (UMI No. 3287936)

Fisette, J. L. & Walton, T. A. (2015). "Beautiful you": Creating contexts for students to become agents of social change. *Journal of Educational Research, 108*(1), 62-76.

Foot, R. E. (2017). *"It's not always what it seems": Exploring the hidden curriculum within a doctoral program.* (Doctoral Dissertation). Retrieved from the ProQuest Dissertation and Theses Global Database. (UMI No. 10645484)

Foreman, L. D. (1984). *Possible effect of the hidden curriculum in American schooling upon the American Indian student* (Doctoral Dissertation). Retrieved from the ProQuest Dissertation and Theses Global Database. (UMI No. 8515257)

Gatto, J. T. (2005). *Dumbing us down: The hidden curriculum of compulsory schooling.* New York (check this): New Society Publishers.

Ghosh, R. (2008). Racism: A hidden curriculum. *Education Canada, 48*(4), 26-29.

Ghourchain, N. G. (1988). *What conceptual framework can be derived from the literature for understanding the hidden curriculum in theory?* (Doctoral Dissertation). Retrieved from the ProQuest Dissertation and Theses Global Database. (UMI No. 8815196)

Gillick, A. (2016). *Revealing the fat experience: A neglected dimension of hidden and outside curriculum.* (Doctoral Dissertation). Retrieved from the ProQuest Dissertation and Theses Global Database. (UMI No. 10295517)

Giroux, H. A. (1978). Developing educational programs: Overcoming the hidden curriculum. *The Clearing House, 52*(4), 148-151.

Giroux, H. A. & Purpel, D. A. (1983). (Eds.). *The hidden curriculum and moral education.* Berkeley, CA: McCutchan Publishing Corporation.

Giroux, H., & Penna, A. (1983). Social education in the classroom: The dynamics of the hidden curriculum. In H. Giroux & D. Purpel. (Eds.). *The hidden curriculum and moral education.* (100-121). Berkeley, CA: McCutchan Publishing Corporation.

Gordon, D. (1982). The concept of the hidden curriculum. *Journal of Philosophy of Education, 16*(2), 187-198.

Green, P. A. (2017). *The stories within our voices: Black males navigation educational achievement* (Doctoral Dissertation). Retrieved from the ProQuest Dissertation and Theses Global Database. (UMI No. 10607343)

Haberman, M. & Bracey, G. W. (1997). The anti-learning curriculum of urban schools: Part, 1, The problem. *Kappa Delta Pi Record, 33*(3), 88-89.

Hall, E. T. (1969). The anthropology of space: an organizing model. In E. T. Hall, *The hidden dimension.* (101-112). Garden City, NY: Anchor Books.

Halstead, M., & Xiao, J. (2010). Values education and the hidden curriculum. In T. Lovat, R. Toomey & N. Clement (Eds.). *International research handbook on values education and student wellbeing* (pp' 303-319). London Springer.

Handy, J. L. (2017). *In search of equity and excellence for Central Valley Education: Teacher educator perceptions of preparing multiple subject preservice teachers.* (Doctoral Dissertation) Retrieved from the ProQuest Dissertation and Theses Global Database (UMI No. 10280584).

Hannay, L. M. (1984). *Cultural reproduction via the hidden curriculum (socialization, instruction) (*Doctoral Dissertation). Retrieved from the ProQuest Dissertation and Theses Global Database. (UMI No. 3287936)

Haralambos, M. & Holborn, M. (1990). *Sociology: Themes and perspectives.* London: Unwin Hyman.

Heilman-Houser, R. A. (1997). *Unintended messages related to issues of equality and diversity in the hidden curriculum* (Doctoral Dissertation). Retrieved from the ProQuest Dissertation and Theses Global Database. (UMI No. 9733734)

Hemmings, A. (2000). The hidden curriculum corridor. *High School Journal, 83*(2), 1-10.

Henson, K. T. (1995). *Curriculum development for educational reform*. New York: HarperCollins.

Henson, K. T. (2006). *Curriculum planning: Integrating multiculturalism, constructivism, and educational reform. 3rd Edition*. Long Grove, IL: Waveland Press, Inc.

Hopman, M., de Winter, M., & Koops, W. (2014). Analyzing the hidden curriculum: A method for the analysis of values in youth care interventions. *European Journal of Research Methods for Behavioral and Social Sciences, 10*(1), 12-20

Horn Jr., R. A. (2003). Developing a critical awareness of the hidden curriculum through media literacy. *Clearing House, 76*(6), 298-300

Jachim. N. (1987). The hidden curriculum. *A Review of General Semantics, 44*(1), 83-85.

Jackson, D. A. O. (2011). *Perceptions of school: Black males in a suburban high school* (Doctoral Dissertation). Retrieved from the ProQuest Dissertation and Theses Global Database. (UMI No. 3460059)

Jackson, P. W. (1968). *Life in classrooms*. New York: Holt, Rinehart and Winston, Inc.

Jackson, P. W. (1992). Conceptions of curriculum and curriculum specialists. In L. E. Beyer, & M.W. Apple (Eds). The curriculum: Problems, politics, and possibilities. (3-40). Albany, NY: State University of New York Press.

Jay, M. (2003). Critical race theory, multicultural education, and the hidden curriculum. *Multicultural Perspectives, 5*(4), 3-9.

Jerald, C. D. (December 2006). Issues Brief. School Culture: "The Hidden Curriculum." Washington, D. C: The Center for Comprehensive School Reform and Improvement. http: www. centerforcsri.org

Johnson, N. B. (1980). The material culture of public school classrooms: The symbolic integration of local schools and national culture. *Anthropology & Education Quarterly, 11*(6), 173-190).

Johnson, N. B. (1982). Education as environmental socialization: Classroom spatial patterns and the transmission of sociocultural norms. *Anthropological Quarterly, 55*(1), 31-43.

Joughin, G. (2010). The hidden curriculum revisited: A critical review of research into the influence of summative assessment on learning. *Assessment and Evaluation in Higher Education, 35*(3), 335-345.

Kentli, F. D. (2009). Comparison of hidden curriculum theories. *European Journal of Educational Studies*, 1(2), 83-88.

Kidd, R. J. M. (1995). *Becoming a woman: Self, world and identity of primary school girls.* (Doctoral Dissertation). Retrieved from the ProQuest Dissertation and Theses Global Database. (UMI No. U077316)

Kohlberg, L. (1983). The moral atmosphere of the school. In H. Giroux & D. Purpel. (Eds.). *The hidden curriculum and moral education.* (61-81). Berkeley, CA: McCutchan Publishing Corporation.

Kohlberg, L. (2003). The cognitive-developmental approach to moral education. In A.C. Ornstein, Behar-Horenstein, L.S. & Pajak, E. F (Eds.). *Contemporary issues in curriculum* (3rd Edition). (16/- 179). Boston: Pearson Education, Inc.

Langhout, R. D., & Mitchell, C. A. (2008) Engaging contexts: Drawing the link between student and teacher experiences of the hidden curriculum. *Journal of Community and Applied Psychology, 18*(6), 593-614.

Lautenbach, C. J. (2004). *What kinds of adolescent leaders are hiding in Newbery books?* (Doctoral Dissertation). Retrieved from the

ProQuest Dissertation and Theses Global Database. (UMI No. 3135101)

LeCompte, M. (1978). Learning to work: The hidden curriculum of the classroom. *Anthropology & Education Quarterly, 9*(1), 22-37.

Leogrande, C. (2001). Beware of literacy software: Connecting with home and school values. In P.R. Schmidt & A. Watts Palliotet *Exploring values through literature, multimedia, and Literacy events.* Newark, DE: International Reading Association.

Lincoln, Y. S. (1992). Curriculum studies and the traditions of inquiry: The humanistic tradition. In L. E. Beyer, & M.W. Apple (Eds). *The curriculum: Problems, politics, and possibilities.* (334-350). Albany, NY: State University of New York Press.

Londot, G. L. (2018). *High school stem teacher perceptions of female student success: A descriptive study.* (Doctoral Dissertation). Retrieved from the ProQuest Dissertation and Theses Global Database. (UMI No. 10821827)

Lutfi, G. A. A.-D. (1990). *Images of males and females in primary and middle school textbooks in Iraq. A content analysis study* (Doctoral Dissertation). Retrieved from the ProQuest Dissertation and Theses Global Database. (UMI No. 9112105)

Macleod, A. (2014). The hidden curriculum: Is it time to re-consider the concept? *Medical Teacher, 36*(6), 539-540

Margolis, E. (Ed.). (2001). *The hidden curriculum in higher education.* London: Routledge.

Margolis, E., Soldatenko, M., Acker, S. & Gair, M. (2001). Peekaboo: Hiding and outing the curriculum. In E. Margolis, *The hidden curriculum in higher education.* (1-20), New York: Routledge.

Marker, G. & Mehlinger, H. (1992). Social studies. In P. W. Jackson, (Ed.). *Handbook of research on curriculum.* (830-851). New York: Macmillan Publishing Company.

Martin, J. (1983). What should we do we a hidden curriculum when we find one? In H. Giroux & D. Purpel. (Eds.). *The hidden curriculum and moral education.* (122-139). Berkeley, CA: McCutchan Publishing Corporation.

Martinson, D. L. (2003). Defeating the "hidden curriculum": Teaching political participation in the social studies classroom. *The Clearinghouse, 76*(3), 132-136.

Martinson, D. L. (1992). The front line: Hazelwood: The end of the "hidden curriculum" charade? *The High School Journal, 75*(3), 131-136.

McCutcheon, G. (1988). Curriculum and the work of teachers. In L. E. Beyer, & M.W. Apple(Eds). *The curriculum: Problems, politics, and possibilities.* (191-203). Albany, NY: State University of New York Press.

McNeil, J. D. (1990). *Curriculum: A comprehensive introduction*: New York: HarperCollins.

Meighan, R. & Harber, C. (2007). *A sociology of educating.* 5th Ed. New York: Continuum.

Meighan, R. & Walker, S. (2007). The hidden curriculum of language. In R. Meighan & C. Harber, *A sociology of educating.* 5th Ed. New York: Continuum.

Mill, M. L. (2017). *Evaluating affective competency in undergraduate nursing: An interpretive description. (Doctoral Dissertation).* Retrieved from the ProQuest Dissertation and Theses Global Database. (UMI No. 10835078)

Munt, G. C. (1991). *Gender bias in textbooks in selected kinesiology courses in Texas colleges and universities.* (Doctoral Dissertation). Retrieved from the ProQuest Dissertation and Theses Global Database. (UMI No. 9201538)

Myles, B.S., Trautman, M. L. & Schelvan, R. L. (2004). *The hidden curriculum: Practical solutions for understanding rules in social situations.* Shawnee Mission, KS: Autism Asperger Publishing Co.

Oliva, P. F. (2005). *Developing the curriculum.* 6th Edition. Boston: Pearson.

Oztok, M. (2013). *The hidden curriculum of online learning. Discourses of Whiteness, social absence, and inequity* (Doctoral Dissertation). Retrieved from the ProQuest Dissertation and Theses Global Database. (UMI No. 3666067)

Petriwskyj, A. (2009). Diversity and inclusion in the early years. *International Journal of Inclusive Education, 14*(2), 195-212.

Porterfield, L. (2013). *Hidden in plain sight: Young Black women, place, and visual culture* (Doctoral Dissertation). Retrieved from the ProQuest Dissertation and Theses Global Database. (UMI No. 3564850)

Posner, G. F. (1988). Models of curriculum planning. In L. E. Beyer, & M.W. Apple (Eds). *The curriculum: Problems, politics, and possibilities.* (77-96). Albany, NY: State University of New York Press.

Previna, D. S. (2011). *Hidden in plain view: Classroom space, teacher agency, and the hidden curricula* (Doctoral Dissertation). Retrieved from the ProQuest Dissertation and Theses Global Database. (UMI No. 3486009)

Prewitt, A. R. (2008). *A study of Georgia's hidden curriculum: Institutional discrimination in the eighth grade* (Doctoral Dissertation). Retrieved from the ProQuest Dissertation and Theses Global Database. (UMI No. 3311301)

Rahman, K. (2013). Belonging and learning to belong in school: The implications of the hidden curriculum for indigenous students. *Discourse: Studies in the Cultural Politics of Education,34*(5), 660-672.

Reisman, A. B. (2006). Outing the hidden curriculum. *Hasting Center Report*. July-August 9. Rodriguez, N. N. (2017). *Hidden in history: Examining Asian American elementary teachers' enactment of Asian American History*. (Doctoral Dissertation). Retrieved from the ProQuest Dissertation and Theses Global Database. (UMI No. 11013253)

Sambell, K., & McDowell, L. (1998). The construction of the hidden curriculum: Messages and meanings in the assessment of student learning. *Assessment and Evaluation in Higher Education, 23*(4), 591-402.

Sari, M. & Doganay, A. (2009). Hidden curriculum on gaining the value of respect for human dignity: A qualitative study in two elementary schools in Adana. *Educational Sciences: Theory and Practice, 9*(2), 925-940.

Semali, L. (2002). (2002 December/January). Crossing the information highway: The web of meaning and bias in global media. *Reading online 6*(5). Available: http://www.readingonline. org/newliteracies/lit_index.asp?HREF=semali3/index.html

Scheepstra, T. (2018). *Making meaning of gender-based violence: Elite subjectivity and gender performance in a Canadian private school*. (Doctoral Dissertation). Retrieved from the ProQuest Dissertation and Theses Global Database. (UMI No. 10937512)

Schubert, W. H. (1986). *Curriculum: Perspective, paradigm, and possibility*. New York: MacMillan.

Shirk, E. (1976). The "hidden curriculum revisited." *Journal of Thought 1*(1), 53-57.

Snyder, B. R. (1971). *The hidden curriculum*. New York: Alfred A. Knopf.

Sockett, H. (1992). The moral aspect of the curriculum. In P. W. Jackson, (Ed.). *Handbook of research on curriculum*. (543-569). New York: Macmillan Publishing Company.

Sosniak, L. A. (2007). The generalist educator: Making a mark on curriculum studies. In D.T. Hansen, M.E. Driscoll, & R. V. Arcilla, *A life in classrooms*. (108-121) New York: Teachers College Press.

Stevens, E. & Woods, G. (Eds). (1987). *Justice, ideology, and education*. New York: Random House

Titman, W. (1994). *Special places; Special people: The hidden curriculum of school grounds*. World Wide Fund for Nature, Toronto, Canada.

Turbes, S., Krebs, E. & Axtell, S. (2002). The hidden curriculum in multicultural medical education: The role of case examples. *Academic Medicine, 77*(3), 209-216.

Vallance, E. (1973). Hiding the hidden curriculum. *Curriculum Theory Network, 4*, 5-21.

Van Walsum, J. (2014). *Visually understanding school grounds: Schooling at its intersection with community and social status* (Doctoral Dissertation). Retrieved from the ProQuest Dissertation and Theses Global Database. (UMI No. 3632760)

Walker, D. (1990). *Fundamentals of curriculum*. Fort Worth, TX: Harcourt Brace College Publishers.

Wiles, J. & Bondi, J. (1993). *Curriculum development: A guide to practice*. (4th edition). New York: Macmillan.

Wren, D. J. (1993). *A comparison of the theories of adolescent moral development of Lawrence Kohlberg and Carol Gilligan: Alternative views of the hidden curriculum* (Doctoral Dissertation). Retrieved from the ProQuest Dissertation and Theses Global Database. (UMI No. 9325972)

Wren, D. J. (1999). School culture: Exploring the hidden curriculum, *Adolescence, 34*(135), 593-596.

THE HIDDEN CURRICULUM: VISUAL/PHOTOGRAPHIC TOOLS TO INTERPRET THE K-12 SCHOOLS' VISUAL MATERIAL CULTURE

Chapter One established the importance of both the K-12 school environment and the messages of the visual material culture regarding diversity. This chapter introduces the concept of nonverbal communication as the mechanism of communication associated with material culture and the tools to read/interpret these messages.

Non-Verbal Communications of the Hidden Curriculum

The link between the material culture of the hidden curriculum and learning from the hidden curriculum involves the mechanism of nonverbal communication (Rapoport, 1982). He notes: "Since environments apparently provide cues for behavior, but do not do it verbally, it follows that they must represent a form of nonverbal behavior" (p. 50). Rapoport goes on to summarize: " . . . environments are more than just inhibiting, facilitating, or even catalytic; they not only remind, they also predict and describe" (p. 77). The material culture of the school classrooms and hallways communicates to the schools' inhabitants via nonverbal communication both the description of and the prescription for the culture. In other words, school values, beliefs, and "how things are thought about around here" are communicated by the classroom and hallway artifacts. The building designs and architecture, art, sculpture, posters, signs, and graffiti all contribute to the telling and reminding of the school culture. The reminding function of the material culture or its mnemonic function is illustrated in Shade Box 2-1. Again, to quote Rapoport:

"The mnemonic function of the environment … reminding people of the behavior expected of them … takes the remembering from the person and places the reminding in the environment" (p. 80–81). In other words, the material culture contains the encoded information of the hidden curriculum, and students and teachers decode the cultural information by mechanism of nonverbal communication. The material culture containing the hidden curriculum teaches; and by the processes of observing and interpreting the teaching, lessons can be deciphered or decoded. And to underscore the thesis of this book—the hidden curriculum in the material culture can be photographed!

Shade Box 2-1: Illustration of Rapoport's Mnemonic Function

THE BUILT ENVIRONMENT: DO IVY WALLS HAVE MEMORIES?

The above question may appear to be a strange one. Certainly, walls do not contain memory cells. Literally there are no "memory storage units" imbedded in the structures of the built environment on college campuses, but the structure and settings of our built environment do appear to "remind" us of certain behaviors. Amos Rapoport (1982) refers to this "reminding" as the mnemonic function of the environment. The environment thus communicates, through a whole set of cues, the most appropriate choices to be made: the cues are meant to elicit appropriate emotions, interpretations, behaviors, and transactions by setting up the appropriate situations and contexts. The environment can thus be said to act as a mnemonic "… it takes the remembering from the person and places the reminding in the environment" (Rapoport, 1982, pp. 80–81). The built environments on our campuses were constructed with encoded messages. When they are decoded through student behavior, a reminding or mnemonic function has occurred. By analyzing the built environments, a more complete understanding can be provided of the student behavior that occurs in these settings as well as a greater understanding of the contribution that environments make to student behavior. In fact, an analysis of the "reminding" given by built environments often produces a different and useful perspective. For example, the growing problem of "rowdy student behavior" at commencement ceremonies can be studied by such an analysis.

Student Commencement Behavior

Over the past few years, there has been an increasing concern expressed by the faculty and administration over the ever-increasing incidents of inappropriate behavior at commencement ceremonies. It is common to hear graduation referred to as the "college circus." Recently, one institution asked a faculty committee to review the deterioration of student commencement behavior and to make recommendations for improvement. During one of the work sessions, one faculty member asked an interesting question. He wondered how each new graduating class could pick up on the previous student commencement behavior, since few undergraduates ever attended a graduation prior to their own. The answer to this question, in part, is that the cues for the inappropriate behavior is in the built environment. The setting "reminds" the student of certain behavior.

It Works This Way!

The commencement exercises for this particular institution (as for most others) are held in the basketball field house. Students are seated by colleges on fold out bleachers next to the court floor. (The same seating as at basketball games.) The physical setting allows the backboards and scoreboards to remain visible, so the seating arrangement cues "sporting behavior" not "graduation behavior." In fact, at one recent commencement ceremony, the students on the south side of the court yelled to their counterparts sitting on the north side: "We've got spirit, how about you?" The students on the north replied in a louder voice: "We've got spirit, HOW ABOUT YOU?" This back and forth volley continued with ever-increasing volume for several minutes.

The above behavior is appropriate for a sporting event but not for commencement exercises. However, the encoded messages of the "built environment" remind students of the yelling and cheering associated with competitive sporting events. In fact, by arranging students by colleges, each with their own banner, "competitive teams" are formed to enhance the rowdiness called for by the field house environment. Institutions that are small enough to still hold commencement in the college chapel probably do not have the rowdy behavior to this extent. The encoded messages in that setting elicit behavior more compatible to the behavior that faculty and administrators are seeking for graduation ceremonies.

Intervention Strategy

By taking into account the mnemonic function, the faculty committee recommended that students should not be seated in the bleachers, but that chairs be placed on the floor. Such an arrangement should cue behaviors that are more "church or meeting" like in nature rather than the "sporting event" behavior. Obviously, many other factors go into student commencement behavior than just the physical setting and the seating arrangement. However, these built environmental factors may be far more important than previously thought.

Ivy Walls: A Final Thought

Bloom (1977) suggests that the upper limit on the ability to predict human behavior solely on the basis of personal characteristics is relatively low. He further suggests that person-only conceptualizations leave perhaps three-quarters of the variation in human behavior unexplained. How much of the variation can be explained by the mnemonic function of the built environment? In the future, perhaps counselors and student personnel workers will be replaced by architects and carpenters! Probably not, but the possibility has some merit. Are we not, now, attending to the many problems produced by earlier architects and carpenters?

Bloom, B. L. (1977). *Community Mental Health*. Monterey, CA: Brooks/Cole Publishing Company.

Rapoport, A. (1982). *The Meaning of the Built Environment: A Nonverbal Communication Approach*. Beverly Hills, CA: Sage Publications.

The Interpretations of Photographs

Why take photographs? There can be many answers to this question, but for the efforts represented in this book, the answer is to find ways to address the negative messages and to enhance the positive messages. The hidden curriculum is a social process and Harper (1989) suggests that these types of processes "can be understood better if frozen in a photographic image" (p. 81). Visual images are critical to the process of understanding the hidden curriculum, but visual images need interpretation. If nonverbal communication is the voice of school artifacts, then the interplay of artifact characteristics and the life experiences of the interpreter becomes a critical factor in understanding the potential messages of the artifacts. The messages are not "fixed" by the material object itself but can vary depending upon the observer's background and their interpretative process. Kaminski and Banning, (2007) noted this relationship: "When an individual views a visual representation, be it a piece of art such as a statue, a poster on the wall, or a design of a building, their beliefs, values, and needs are factors that determine how the message is comprehended" (p. 109).

Different viewers, for example students, teachers, and administrators, can have different interpretations. The decoding process includes both the artifact and its encoded messages and the values and life experiences of the observer/photographer. Rather than seeing the multiple interpretations as a "threat to validity" of the messages, I take a more postmodern stance and see the multiple interpretations contributing to a richer discussion of the meaning of the artifact.

Tools for Interpretation of Photographs: An Eclectic Approach

The next sections of this chapter provide tools for understanding an eclectic and practical approach to interpreting the photographs of the school's hidden curriculum. This eclectic approach is built around the process of asking questions of the material culture of interest. Answers to the following questions help in providing the information needed for forming the interpretation of the artifact message. These questions can be viewed in a postmodern perspective as tools for deconstruction of the images. The interpretative frame is designed around asking the following questions.

Basic Question: Manifest or Latent?

First, there is the basic question of whether the message of the artifact is manifest or latent (Neuendorf, 2000). If manifest, then few interpretive questions need to be asked. The message is self-evident and obvious. It is the denotation of the image, but if the message is more latent or hidden, then additional questions are needed to help the interpretation. Kaminski and Banning (2007) state: "The latent content is covert; it is the connotation of the image and interpretative strategies that come into play" (p. 109). The more the images fall in the direction of latent/connotative the greater the need for interpretive skills. While the concepts manifest and latent and others that follow are presented as dichotomies/binaries, they should be treated as "fuzzy" and not "crisp" (Ragin, 2008). There is considerable overlap between and among the question categories, and multiple questions are often needed to form the interpretation of the image.

Additional Questions: Tools for Deconstruction.

Does the photograph of the cultural artifact contain binary oppositions?

Look for arrangement of elements in pairs (Emmison & Smith, 2000). For example, male vs. female, old vs. young, and myriad of other possibilities exist. The following are questions stemming from the binary perspective that I have found particularly useful in my interpretative process.

What is the relationship among the elements in the photograph in terms of foreground and background?

The more "important" elements of the photograph appear as the foreground. For example, in many photographs of poster materials, men/boys appear in the foreground and women/girls in the background. If the photo includes more than one race or ethnicity, then often the White figures are in the foreground and persons of color are in the background. If multiple roles are depicted in the photograph, then you often find the most important role in the foreground and less important roles in the background. A related tool is the concept of juxtaposition. How are the elements in the photo positioned to each other?

What is the relationship among the people in the photograph in terms of body position?

Messages of power in photographs are communicated by body position (Branaman, 2001; Emmison & Smith, 2000). Typically, the person standing is associated with more power than those sitting (Banning, Sexton, Most, & Maier, 2007). For example, photographs of office settings often show the male figure standing over the female working at a desk. Teachers are most often seen as standing in a classroom while students are seated.

What is the relationship among the overt public messages given via institutional publications, such as institutional mission statements, website material and the messages found in the school's cultural artifacts?

For example, many schools use photographs of groups of students engaged in a variety of activities that include a diverse student group, for example school field trips. However, if you go to the departments, they often have posted their activities like field trips, etc., but seldom do you find the mix of students like those in the school's website. Schools often promote special programs like STEM or science programs for girls. Again, if you go to the science classrooms, you do not find the theme being portrayed in local artifacts like posters. The binary of what is being promoted by the school and what is being done in the classroom is clearly present.

What roles are depicted in the artifact photograph and to which person characteristics are they assigned? What roles are missing for specific groups?

From my experience, many motivational posters directed toward African American students have the students holding a basketball, suggesting that the path forward for Black students is athletics only. However, posters that depict science roles are often represented by males only. In other words, many photographs of cultural artifacts carry the messages from the hidden curriculum of vocational stereotyping.

What symbols and associated meanings are included in the artifact photograph?

The artifacts of school material culture send symbolic messages (Gagliardi, 1990). Formal entrances to schools can suggest the cultural message of strength. These are most often found as part of the architectural structure of doors to the school's administrative offices. Restroom symbols suggest the school's position regarding many gender issues. These are just a couple of examples as there are a myriad of possibilities within the K-12 school environment.

Does the artifact photograph suggest a narrative? Does the photograph or many times the series of photographs tell a story?

Is there a storyline (Emmison and Smith, 2000)? For example, often classrooms will have a series of murals or posters depicting the history of a subject matter. Within the series there are often stories imbedded regarding gender and race. The role of women can often be found in the "series of leadership" photographs depicting previous principals and superintendents posted on school hallways. Do women appear in the series of leadership photographs? When do they appear? What is their role? These observations can lead to the narrative or story of school or district female leadership.

Do the elements of the "Behavioral/Physical Traces" observational method (Zeisel, 1975, 1981, 2006) help in the interpretation of the cultural artifact?

The behavioral trace method is built on the notion that as we use cultural artifacts in our environment, traces of that use or behavior can be detected. These behavioral traces can be interpreted as non-verbal messages that increase the understanding of the hidden curriculum and can be photographed (Banning, 1988). Zeisel's work focuses on four types of behavioral and physical trace categories. The by-product of use category includes the messages of erosion, leftovers, missing traces, and accretions. The category of adaptation of use captures how the artifacts of the school are moved, connected, and separated by behavioral use. The third category is displays of self, which captures how we use the physical artifacts for the processes of personalization, identification, and communicating group membership. Finally, the last category is public messages. Three types of messages are described: official, unofficial, and illegitimate. (See Appendix B for a full description of Zeisel's observational method with examples and photo illustrations.)

Summary

Visual research opens the door to an important path to understanding a K-12 school's hidden curriculum. The messages of the buildings, art, posters, symbols and signs, and other components of the school's material culture can be captured by photographs allowing for the use of interpretative tools to tease out possible important teachings of the hidden curriculum. Chapter Three will include illustrations of these interpretative tools focusing on diversity. With the illustrations will be my interpretations—unavoidable given the interpretative process discussed in this chapter.

References

Banning, J. H. (1988) Behavioral traces: A concept for campus ecologists. *The Campus Ecologist,* 6(2),1,3.

Banning, J. H., Sexton, J., Most, D. E., & Maier, S. (2007). Gender asymmetries encountered in the search and exploration of mining engineering program web sites: A portrayal of posture and roles. *Journal of Women and Minorities in Science and Engineering,* 13 (2), 165-174.

Branaman, A. (Ed.). (2001). *Self and society.* New York: Blackwell Publishers.

Emmison, M. & Smith, P. (2000). *Researching the visual.* London: Sage Publications.

Gagliardi, P. (Ed.). (1990). *Symbols and artifacts: Views of the corporate landscape.* New York: Aldine de Gruyter.

Harper, D. (1989). Visual sociology: Expanding sociological vision. In G. Banks, J.L.

McCartney, and E. Brent (Eds). *New technology in sociology: Practical applications in research and work.* New Brunswick, NJ: Transaction Publishers.

Kaminski, K. & Banning, J. H. (2007). Visuals in public places: Whose interpretation is it? In R. E. Griffin, M. D. Averinou, & J. Gieson (Eds). *History, community and culture: Celebrating tradition and transforming the future* (pp. 109-114). Madison, WI: IDEC

Neuendorf, K. A. (2000). *The content analysis guidebook.* Thousand Oaks: CA: Sage Publications.

Ragin, C. C. (2008). *Redesigning social inquiry: Fuzzy sets and beyond.* Chicago, IL: Chicago University Press.

Rapoport, A. (1982). *The meaning of the built environment: A nonverbal communications approach.* Beverly Hills, CA: Sage Publications.

Zeisel, J. (1975). *Sociology and architectural design.* New York: Russell Sage Foundation.

Zeisel, J. (1981). *Inquiry by design.* Monterey, CA: Brooks/Cole.

Zeisel, J. (2006). *Inquiry by design: Environment/behavior/ neuroscience in architecture, interiors, landscape, and planning.* New York: W. W. Norton & Company.

PHOTOGRAPHING K-12 SCHOOL DIVERSITY MESSAGES

What I Bring to the Interpretative Process

Illustrations of interpreting school artifacts focusing on diversity will follow in this chapter. Ideology not only influences the interpretation of images, as noted in Chapter Two, but it also guides the camera. The camera does not take pictures, the photographers do—they choose what to photograph suggesting they have an interpretation of why the photo is important. Given the importance of what the observer brings to the interpretative process, I have provided a brief overview of what I bring to the observation/interpretative process regarding diversity (see Shade Box 3-1). Chapter Three will include illustrations of the interpretative tools from Chapter Two focusing on diversity. With the illustrations will be my interpretations—unavoidable given the interpretative process. It is incumbent that I make known what I bring to the observing, photographing, and interpretative process for finding meaning in the material culture of K-12 schools relating to diversity. The following is a summary of my thoughts that I bring to the interpretative process regarding school diversity.

Shade Box 3.1: My Interpretative Stance on Diversity

Diversity has many meanings. The following definition by Winkle-Wagner and Locks (2017) captures the foundation of how it is used within this manuscript and my interpretive stance:

" . . . we focus particularly on diversity as it relates to those students who have historically been excluded, marginalized, or disallowed from participation in postsecondary institutions because of their racial or ethnic background" (p.xii).

To this foundation of exclusion, marginalization, and disallowed participation, issues related to gender, sexual orientation, disabilities, and religion are also included in my use of the concept of diversity. The importance of engaging all students with full participation within the institutional fabric is of critical importance to student success (Quaye & Harper, 2015).

Important Conceptual Frameworks

There are several important conceptual frameworks and related scholarship that help shape and guide my thinking about diversity: Nancy Fraser's framework of redistribution, recognition, affirmation, and transformation relating to "parity of participation" (2003), James Banks's (2003) framework for understanding approaches to multicultural education and curriculum reform, and Peggy McIntosh's (1989) discussion of privilege.

Summary of the Conceptual Frameworks

Embracing the concept of diversity requires parity of participation, and social justice requires arrangements that permit its members to interact with one another as equals (Fraser & Honneth, 2003). Two conditions prevent "parity of participation" (Fraser & Honneth, 2003, pp. 10–11): (1) Issue of redistribution (the current distribution of resources, wealth, education, health care, and other assets) presents equal participation. (2) Issue of recognition [the disrespect of identities and pressures to assimilate to dominate cultural norms (white male privilege) and the marginalization of racial, ethnic, gender, sexual, and ideological minorities] prevents equal participation. Two strategies are necessary to address non-parity of participation (Fraizer & Honneth, 2003): (A) Affirmative strategies that involve addressing and correcting the outcomes of injustices, and (B) Transformative strategies that address injustices by restructuring the underlying cultural/social/political framework. I will term this framework the privilege structure that exists. Blackmore (2016) provides an overview of Fraser's work in relation to educational leadership. Education leadership and curriculum reform/transformation are critical to these strategies (Banks, 2003) as is the understanding of privilege (McIntosh, 1989; Middleton, Anderson, & Banning, 2009).

My Thoughts on Diversity and Organizations

For me, the diversity challenge of parity of participation in organization relates directly to the privilege structure of White male gender. In weaving the following relationship between male gender and organizational behavior, the complexity of the relationship has been simplified in order to highlight the patterns. Several authors have provided, for me, key definitional elements for understanding gender and organizations. The following books are noted: Elizabath Dodson Grey's (1982) *Patriarch as a Conceptual Trap*; Ann Wilson Schaef (1985), who wrote *Women's Reality: An Emerging Female System in a White Male Society*, and Alfie Kohn (1992), the author of *No Contest: The Case Against Competition*. Each of these authors presents a set of myths that provide the socialization blueprint for gender roles in our society and the foundation for the white male system. Elizabeth Dodson Gray (1982) suggests three myths: (a) reality is construed to be hierarchical: To reinforce the construction of a hierarchical reality everything in our society is ranked from the top twenty-five in various sporting events to the top pizza parlors in town. Ranking, according to Kohn (1986), is our national pastime; (b) man is above nature: Man or more specifically "men" are on top of the hierarchy and control nature. They assume dominion over nature and use it for their purposes. Forests are cleared, dams are built, and the earth is plowed; and (c) nature is feminine: If nature is feminine, then it follows that our metaphors and analogies for nature are feminine: for example, Mother Nature, virgin forests, and raping the land. It also follows that if "men" control nature, then they control women. These three myths provide the hierarchical structure necessary for the domination of women and nature by men. Nowhere is this hierarchical structure so ingrained and more powerful than in organizations, including colleges and university. Ann Wilson Schaef (1985) suggests four myths that guide the gender socialization process: (a) the white male system is the only thing that exists; (b) the white male system is innately superior; (c) the white male system knows and understands everything; and (d) the white male system believes that it is possible to be totally logical, rational, and objective. These myths reinforce the notion that it is indeed the male gender that is on top of the hierarchy and is in control of the internal functioning of the organization. Finally, Alfie Kohn (1986) suggests four myths that strike at the heart of what makes the white male system function: (a) competition is an unavoidable fact of life and part of human nature; (b) competition motivates man to do his best; (c) competition provides a way to have fun and a good time; and (d) competition builds character and is good for self-confidence. Although these competition myths are generally thought to be true by many, they are not supported by social/psychological research. Taken as a whole, these three authors' myths provide the structure for the male socialization blueprint in our society. The myths underpin how males are socialized, how males are supposed to behave in organizations, and "how the organizational system" works in our society. The photographs that follow in this chapter were taken from the foregoing interpretative frame and from my personal experiences as a White, heterosexual, cisgender, abled-bodied, professional, middle-class male.

References

Banks, J. (2003). *An introduction to multicultural education.* 3rd ed. Boston: Allyn & Bacon.

Blackmore, J. (2016). *Educational leadership and Nancy Fraser (Critical studies in educational leadership, management, and administration).* London: Routledge.

Fraser, N., & Honneth, A. (2003). *Redistribution or recognition? A political-philosophical exchange.* London: Verso Publisher.

Grey, E. D. (1982). *Patriarch as a conceptual trap.* Wellesley, MA: Roundtable Press.

Kohn, A. (1992). *No contest: The case against competition.* Boston, MA: Houghton Miffin.

McIntosh, P. (1989 July/August). White privilege. Unpacking the invisible backpack. *Peace and Freedom,* 8-10.

Middleton, V., Anderson, S., & Banning, J. (2009). The journey to understanding privilege: A meta-narrative approach. *Journal of Transformative Education,* 7(4), 294-311.

Quaye, S. J., & Harper, S. R. (Eds.). (2015). *Student engagement in higher education: Theoretical perspectives and practical approaches for diverse populations.* 2nd Ed. New York: Routledge.

Schaef, A. W. (1985). *Women's reality: An emerging female system in a white male society.* San Francisco, CA: Harper & Row.

Winkler-Wagner, R., & Locks, A. M. (2014). *Diversity and inclusion on campus: Supporting racially and ethnically underrepresented students.* New York: Routledge.

Using the Eclectic Interpretative Frame for Understanding Diversity Messages

As noted in Chapter Two, the eclectic interpretative approach provides tools for understanding and interpreting the photographs of school material culture that contributes to the hidden curriculum. Implementation of this approach in this chapter is built around the

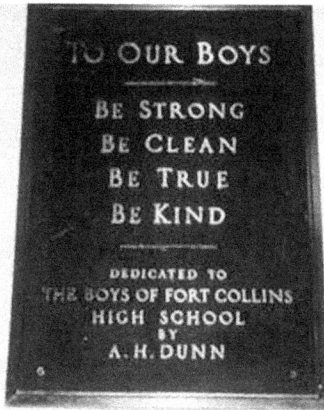

Photo 3.0 Manifest Gender Roles for Boys

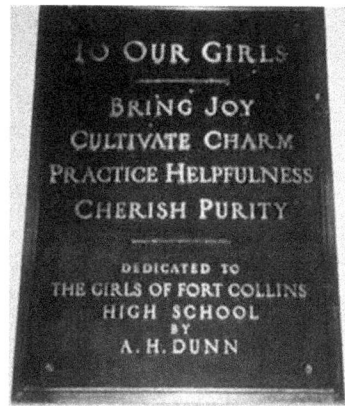

Photo 3.1 Manifest Gender Roles for Girls

process of asking questions of the school's material culture of interest regarding diversity. Answers to the following questions help in providing the information needed for forming the interpretation of the artifact and its relation to the messages of diversity. As noted in Chapter Two, the interpretative frame regarding school diversity is designed around asking the following questions.

Basic Question: Are the Diversity Messages Manifest or Latent?

First, there is the basic question of whether the message of the artifact is manifest or latent (Neuendorf, 2002). If manifest, then few interpretive questions need to be asked. The message is self-evident and obvious. Photos 3.0 and 3.1 were posted next to the principal's office in the school hallway and are clearly manifest. There is no need for further interpretive questions. The hidden curriculum regarding gender roles is in plain sight. Strength is associated with boys and helpfulness with girls. The more the images fall in the direction of latent/connotative the greater the need for interpretive skills. Photos 3.3 and 3.4 are from an elementary school and need only a bit more interpretation. The figures in Photo 3.2 identifies the boy's restroom and 3.3 the girl's restroom in an elementary school.

*Photo 3.2 Latent Gender
Roles for Boys*

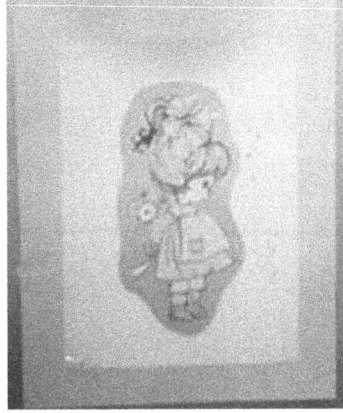

*Photo 3.3 Latent Gender
Roles for Girls*

However, the restroom symbols also communicate gender roles. On close examination, we find more than room identification messages. The boy is shown as active, has eye contact, and perhaps even a job in newspaper delivery. This is in sharp contrast to the girl on the female restroom door. She looks passive and demure. Her head is cast downward, hands behind her back, and no eye contact. She is in pink and holding flowers and appears to be wearing perhaps an apron. These messages, although latent, give clear gender messages reflecting stereotypical roles—a message from the hidden curriculum to support the gender messages of Photos 3.0 and 3.1.

Additional Questions: Tools for Deconstruction

Does the photograph of the cultural artifact contain binary oppositions?

To answer this first question, look for arrangement of elements in pairs (Emmison & Smith, 2000). Both the foregoing manifest and latent photos regarding gender are binary—boys in contrast to girls. Often the binary elements are contained in the same artifact

Photo 3.4 Binary Gender Roles

photograph. For example, in Photo 3.4 a male vs. female binary is presented. Again, the males are pictured as active and involved and the females are in the background as "cheerleaders." Again, this is a strong message from the hidden curriculum within a K-12 hallway mural.

What is the relationship among the elements in the photograph in terms of foreground and background?

The more "important" elements of the photograph appear as the foreground. Using Photo 3.4 again, we have active men involved in multiple roles—comedian, baseball player, football player, movie star, and rock star. In the background, we have women/girls playing only one role—cheerleader.

What is the relationship among the people in the photograph in terms of body position and/or size?

Messages of power in photographs are communicated by body position (Branaman, 2001; Emmison & Smith, 2000). Typically, the person standing is associated with more power than those sitting (Banning, Sexton, Most, & Maier, 2007). Size of the figures within a photograph of an artifact can also suggest power differential. In

Photo 3.5 of a display welcoming students, the large bust is of Abraham Lincoln, a powerful and notable figure in American history, but the female figure is much smaller and presented as a doll-like cheerleader.

Photo 3.5 Differential Size and Role

What is the relationship among the overt public messages given via institutional publications, for example, institutional advertisements, mission statements, recruitment materials, etc., and the messages found in the cultural artifacts?

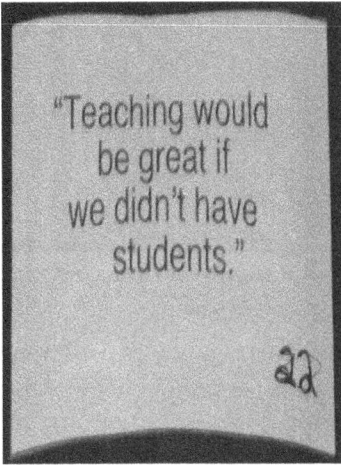

"Teaching would be great if we didn't have students."

Photo 3.6 Photo of Artifact from Teachers' Lounge

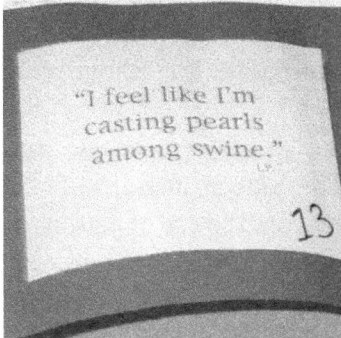

"I feel like I'm casting pearls among swine."

Photo 3.7 Photo of Artifact from Teachers' Lounge

Many schools use websites to promote the value of their schools, often regarding special programs as well as promotional pictures and text highlighting positive student and teacher relationships. These are the overt public messages. Photos 3.6 and 3.7 clearly suggest different than positive messages regarding teachers' views on students. Even though these artifacts were found in the teachers' lounge and perhaps posted as "comic relief," they can be seen as part of the hidden curriculum of attitudes toward all students. Diversity students who may, from other messages in the hidden curriculum, feel marginalized are not comforted by these messages. Faculty lounges are seldom hidden from students.

What roles are depicted in the artifact photograph and to what person are they assigned? What roles are missing for specific groups?

The previous pictures in this chapter clearly illustrate that the messages in many of the photographed artifacts relate to roles for gender. Roles in regard to race can also be found in the photographs of the hidden curriculum. The most often found message in the hidden curriculum for African American youth is "your future is in basketball." In Photo 3.8, the student of color is taller, is holding a

Photo 3.8 Student of Color and Athletics

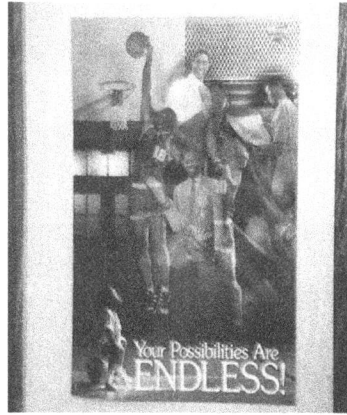

Photo 3.9 Student of Color and Basketball

gym bag, and is wearing a jersey. This message is repeated in Photo 3.9. The poster reads "Your Possibilities are ENDLESS!" Within the poster is a young boy sitting on a basketball looking at "possibilities," and three out of six adults pictured are basketball players. The message is—if you are an African American in our school, your best future possibility is athletics. This not only limits the possibilities for the students, it perpetuates a stereotypic message. Photo 3.10 sends a similar message. The poster is promoting the school value of "PRACTICE SPORTSMANSHIP." This is a school value that

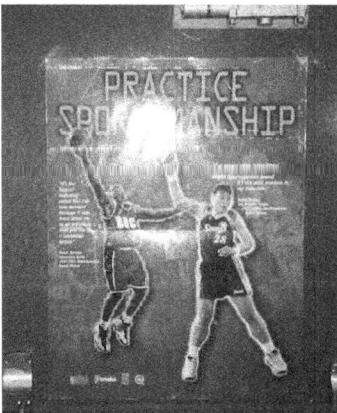

Photo 3.10 Students of Color and Athletics

you expect schools to endorse and promote. The hidden message of this poster stems from the use of persons of color to promote athletics. Again, this is a detrimental message for students of color and the school.

What symbols and associated meanings are included in the artifact photograph?

The artifacts of hidden curriculum send symbolic messages (Gagliardi, 1990). The photo 3.11 of the poster "We all have feelings" is an example of what appears to be a positive poster, but

Photo 3.11 Feeling Symbols

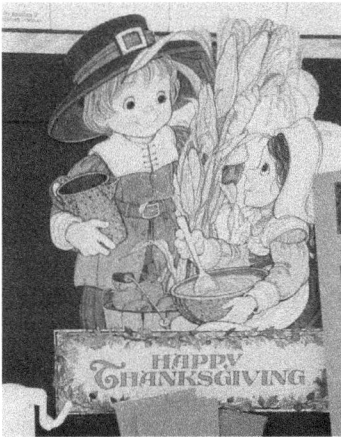

Photo 3.12 Gender Storyline

the "feelings" noted in the poster are associated with different races to produce symbolic associations. The Anglo students in the poster are associated with the symbols (words) "happy," "proud," and "surprised." The one that is presented as a Black student is associated with the symbol "afraid." Two other students in the poster that appear to be students of color are presented as symbols of "angry" and "jealous."

Does the artifact photograph suggest a narrative?

Does the photograph or the series of photographs tell a story? Is there a storyline (Emmison & Smith, 2000)? Photo 3.12 tells the story of Thanksgiving and includes hidden messages regarding gender in the storyline. The male (standing/power) is bringing in the products from farming (active/breadwinner) and the female (sitting/less powerful position) is cooking (stereotypical role).

Do the elements of the "Behavioral/Physical Traces" observational method (Zeisel, 1975, 1981, 2006) help in the interpretation of the cultural artifact?

The behavioral trace method is built on the notion that as we use cultural artifacts in our environment there are traces of that use or behavior which can be detected. These behavioral traces can be interpreted as non-verbal messages that increase the understanding of student behavior and can be photographed (Banning, 1988). Zeisel's work focuses on four types of behavioral/physical trace categories. The by-product of use category includes the messages of erosion, leftovers, missing traces, and accretions. For example, the missing traces concept is also useful in developing interpretation. Often members of diversity groups are missing in campus flyers and other printed material. The category of adaptation of use shows how the artifacts of the school are moved, connected, and separated by behavioral use.

The third category is displays of self that captures how we use the physical artifacts in the processes of personalization, identification, and communicating group membership. Finally, the last category is public messages. Three types of messages are described: official, unofficial, and illegitimate. The category of illegitimate includes graffiti. Graffiti is the most prevalent and often contains the most negative and hurtful diversity messages.

(See Appendix A for a full description of the Zeisel observational method with non-diversity related examples and photo illustrations.)

Moving from Individual Photos to Cultural Themes

Developing an understanding of school cultural themes from a group of individual photographs is basically a task of qualitative data analysis. In qualitative data analysis, the approach of moving from observational data to larger themes falls within two major strategies: inductive and deductive. The inductive approach is a data-driven approach where the movement to larger themes is built on assigning codes/labels to individual data and then comparing the codes to move up the ladder of abstraction to reach themes (Corbin & Strauss, 2008). The deductive approach brings to the observational data categories/themes already having been established by previous research or theory (Boyatzis, 1998). Useful to developing themes from individual photographs is using a combination of both the inductive and the deductive strategies. This combination strategy is termed template analysis (King, 1998). In this approach, deductive or prior codes/categories are established, but inductive or codes driven by the data, are added as needed.

Taxonomies are useful tools in establishing prior codes/categories to assist in moving from the individual photos to cultural themes. The concept of taxonomy is typically noted as stemming from Greek concepts of denoting a method of arranging and is used today to describe a method to group things together. The purpose of a taxonomy (Milgram & Kishino, 1994) is to present an ordered classification system that allows and promotes discussions that can be focused, developments evaluated, research conducted, and data meaningfully compared. Taxonomies can be developed inductively, or if they exist, they can be imported from previous scholarship/research or theory.

Banning and Bartels (1997) developed a taxonomy for classifying diversity artifact messages. This taxonomy has four dimensions: (1) The content of the message; (2) The evaluative impact of the message; (3) Multicultural groups; and (4) The type of physical artifact sending the message. By using this classification taxonomy, each photograph of school physical artifacts can be assigned to a cell in the taxonomy and the questions of which artifacts are communicating what message to what groups with what results can be addressed. The categories for content of photographic messages in Banning and Bartels taxonomy include: (1) Messages of belonging; (2) Messages of safety; (3) Messages of equality; and (4) Messages regarding roles. The artifacts may send multiple messages, and a single photograph may belong to more than one category. The evaluative impact dimension of photographs included two categories: (1) overtly negative and (2) overtly positive. The multicultural group dimension included: (1) gender; (2) race and ethnicity; (3) ethnicity; (4) religion; and (5) sexual orientation. The type of artifacts generating the messages included: (1) architecture: physical structures and design elements of the school; (2) art: including paintings, murals, posters; (3) signs: signs fall within several categories, including official signs, unofficial signs, and illegitimate signs; (3) graffiti: often viewed as an illegitimate sign, but because of its ubiquitous nature on school campuses, it is given separate status in the classification system.

In 2008, the Banning and Bartels taxonomy's category of evaluative content of the message was expanded to include the following evaluations: negative, null, contributive, and transformational (Banning, Middleton, & Dennison, 2008). The negative label is assigned to both manifest and latent photographs where the message is clearly discriminatory and produces a hostile climate for students of diversity. The null category was derived from the work of Freeman (1979) and Betz (1989) and captures the circumstances where a school has an absence of negative, but yet no positives. Apple (1971) supports this view of the null environment regarding the hidden curriculum. Without affirming and sending positive messages, the school does not remain neutral. This is like the concept of "white silence" (DiAngelo, 2016). Being ignored or left out creates a negative environment not from what is said but from what is not said. The contributive and transformational categories were built on the work of Banks (2003). The contributive category captures positive messages, but the messages are presented without the call for personal involvement to bring about change. The placement of a Martin Luther King portrait in the school library certainly sends a positive message and contributes to diversity, but it does not call for personal involvement or discussion with others. The transformative message is also positive but calls for a personal commitment to transform school culture. For example, a poster inviting students to a diversity workshop as well as providing the necessary information to become involved could be categorized as transformative.

Another variation of a taxonomy built on the previous two by Strange and Banning (2015) theorizes that for students to be successful in their educational experience, they should feel welcomed, safe, included, and therefore, a part of the educational community. The notions of welcoming, safety, inclusion, and community become the artifact messages critical to the success of students. Figure 1 presents a matrix for K-12 that helps to expose the diversity-related artifacts of the hidden curriculum. It is like the previous description but includes a category of general diversity and class within the diversity parameter dimension, and the artifact message content includes the messages of inclusion, safety, future role, and person characteristics.

In summary, each picture of an artifact type (art, signs, graffiti, and architecture) would fit into one or more of the cells of the taxonomy (see Figure 1). The taxonomy includes the equity groups to which the artifact message references (general diversity, gender, race/ethnicity, sexual orientation, physical disability, and class), the content of the message includes (inclusion issues, safety issues, future roles, and person characteristics), and the evaluative assessment dimension is represented by the evaluative concepts of negative, null, contributions/additive, and transformational/social action. Photos illustrating the use of the matrix for hidden curriculum artifacts follow in the next section.

A Taxonomy for K-12 Hidden Curriculum Artifacts
Type of Artifact

A r t   S i g n s   G r a f f i t i   A r c h i t e c t u r e

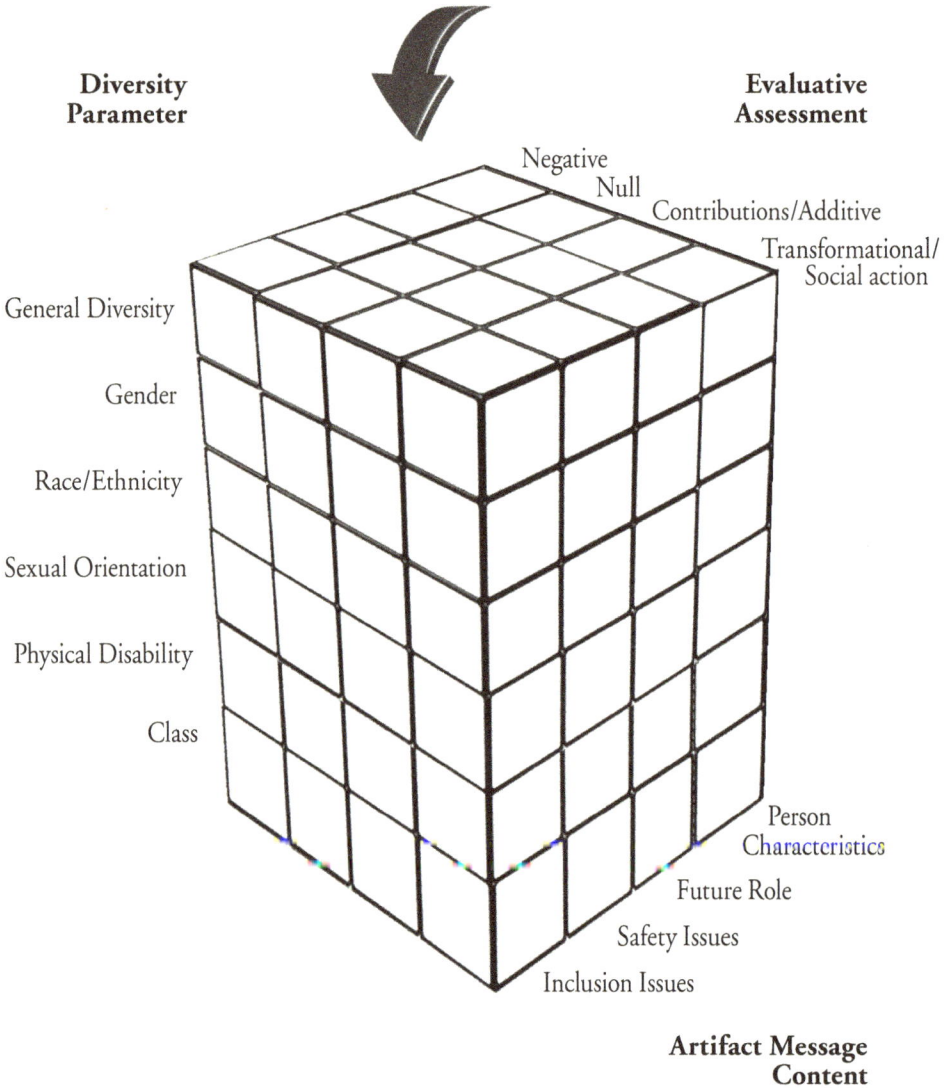

Diversity
Parameter

Evaluative
Assessment

Negative
Null
Contributions/Additive
Transformational/
Social action

General Diversity

Gender

Race/Ethnicity

Sexual Orientation

Physical Disability

Class

Person
Characteristics
Future Role
Safety Issues
Inclusion Issues

Artifact Message
Content

A Taxonomy for K-12 Hidden Curriculum Artifacts: Illustrations

The *Taxonomy for K-12 Hidden Curriculum Artifacts* contains three dimensions and fourteen categories within the dimensions. This three-dimensional space produces 96 cells, and each cell can be described using the fourteen categories within the dimensions of the matrix. For example, if the photograph is of an African American student sitting alone in a crowded cafeteria, it could be placed in the matric cell defined by *Race/Ethnicity – Negative – Inclusion Issues*. Often photographs have multiple messages; therefore, the photographs can fit into more than one cell of the matrix. If the African American student had a basketball next to their lunchbox, then the photo could also be placed in the cell defined by *Race/Ethnicity – Negative – Future Role*. In other words, the cells are fuzzy and not crisp (Ragin, 2008). Using many of the photographs already presented in this manuscript plus a few additional ones, examples of selected cells follow for illustration.

Diversity in General – Contribution/Additive – Inclusion Issues

The following photos (3.13, 3.14, 3.15, 3.16, & 3.17) all send, in general, inclusive messages regarding diversity by supporting the ideals of valuing differences, friendship, and togetherness. While these are positive messages, the focus on the general notion of diversity often does not speak strongly to specific diversity groups. For example, the group posters (3.16 & 3.17) do not specifically show the inclusion of physically disabled students in wheelchairs. Positive diversity posters certainly help send messages counter to the many negative poster messages, but they can also, on close examination, be repeating negative messages for other groups.

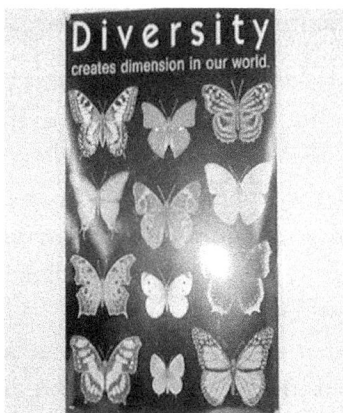

*Photo 3.13 General Diversity-
Contributive/Additive -
Inclusion*

*Photo 3.14 General Diversity-
Contributive/Additive -
Inclusion*

*Photo 3.15 General Diversity -
Contributive/Additive - Inclusion*

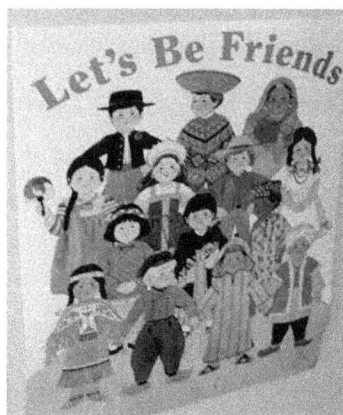

*Photo 3.16 General Diversity -
Contributive/Additive -
Inclusion*

*Photo 3.17 General Diversity -
Contributive/Additive - Inclusion*

Gender – Negative – Personal Characteristics

Female images in posters and artwork often carry hidden messages of personal/group characteristics. These messages for K-12 girls are easily found in previous photographs (cover photo, 3.0, 3.1, 3.2, 3.3, 3.4, & 3.5): that girls are weaker, girls need help, girls are deferential, girls are in the background as cheerleaders, and girls have less power. Photos 3.18 and 3.19 also present a characteristic often found in the hidden gender messages: Females are sexual objects. Photo 3.18 is inviting the K-12 school to bid on "hotties" for dates. Ironically, the proceeds of the bidding process are being sent to a shelter program for battered women. The conflict between the sexism message and the call to help battered women is evidence that messages in the hidden curriculum receive little attention from school personnel.

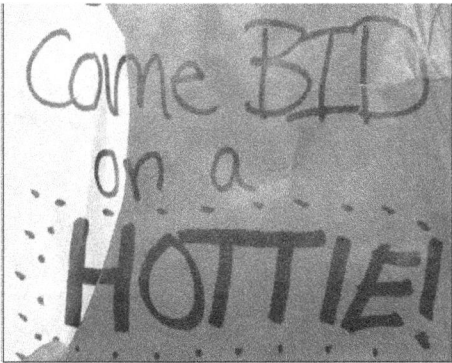

Photo 3.18 Gender - Negative - Personal Characteristics

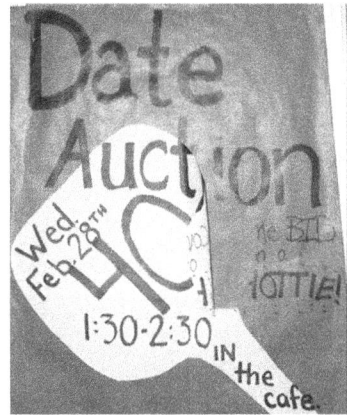

Photo 3.19 Gender - Negative-Personal Characteristics

Gender – Additive/Celebration – Personal Characteristics

The messages within posters can also be positive for gender. Photo 3.20 presents a female student celebrating a positive school experience, underscoring the message that with "studying," success for girls is possible. This message contrasts with those presented in the cell of gender-negative-personal characteristics. The female student is shown achieving success for celebration without the help of a male student.

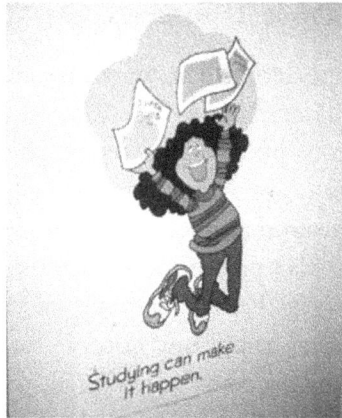

Photo 3.20 Gender – Additive/
Celebration – Personal
Characteristics

Gender – Negative – Future Roles

Photo 3.21 sends messages regarding future roles for boys and girls. Not only is the current computer activity possibly under the supervision of a male, but the future holds a much different picture of how the computer will be used in future occupations. Male careers in the "future bubbles" include athletics, science, and business (even showing a male supervising a female). In contrast, the future career roles for women are the typical stereotypes of nursing, communications, cooking, and dispatcher. The message of "you can do anything" appears to be restricted to gender stereotypes.

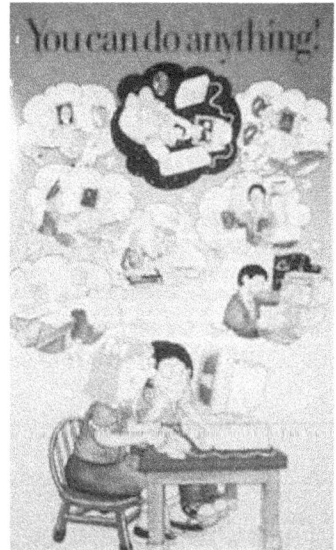

Photo 3.21 Gender - Negative
- Future Roles

Gender – Race/Ethnicity – Negative – Characteristics (American Indian)

Photos 3.22, 3.23, and 3.24 are all photographs taken at a high school, and they represent the "Indians" as the mascot for the school and its athletic teams. Pewewardy (2000), in his article "Why Educators should not Ignore Indian Mascots," underscores the racist messages in the use of the Indian mascot. He points out that the mascots become associated with the American stereotypes of the American Indian culture: Indian men often portrayed in violent images and Indian women as "Pocahontas, . . . Cherokee princess" (p. 4). The three photographs (3.22, 3.23, & 3.24) clearly represent these stereotypes.

Photo 3.22 Race/Ethnicity - Negative - Characteristics (American Indian)

Photo 3.23 Race/Ethnicity - Negative - Characteristics (American Indian)

Photo 3.24 Race/Ethnicity - Negative - Characteristics (American Indian)

Race/Ethnicity – Negative – Future Roles

Photos 3.25 and 3.26, along with previous photos (3.8, 3.9, & 3.10), clearly point out a major diversity message in K-12 material artifacts that current and future roles for the African American male is basketball. This cultural stereotype is being communicated visually in school classrooms and hallways.

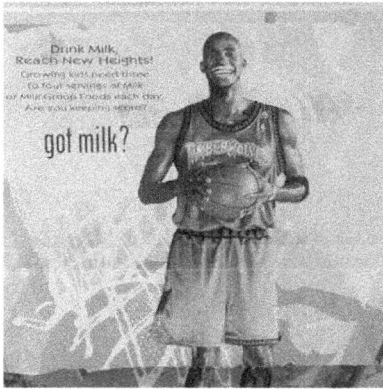

Photo 3.25 Race/Ethnicity - Negative - Future Roles

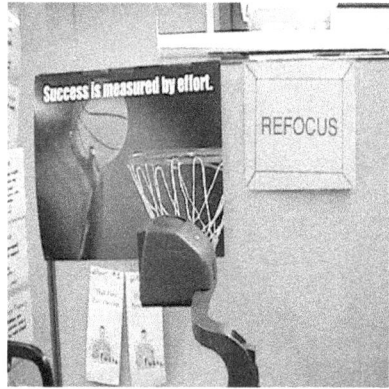

Photo 3.26 Race/Ethnicity - Negative - Future Roles

Gender (non-binary) – Null – No content (no photographs)

K-12 school posters assume gender is binary, and there is no presentation in the material artifacts supportive of transgender and non-conforming gender students. A null or no message of support in the school for non-binary students has negative impact on their development and learning.

Physical Disability – Negative – Inclusion

K-12 students with physical disabilities that require assistive equipment are seldom included in school visual artifacts. The poster in Photo 3.27 is attempting to send a positive diversity message, but it fails to include the message that disabled students in chairs also smile. Photo 2.28 shows an arrangement of materials needed for future admissions to college, but the arrangement makes it impossible for many disabled students to acquire—they are too high, above a

Photo 3.27 Physical Disability - Negative - Inclusion

Photo 3.28 Physical Disability - Negative - Inclusion

heater, and behind a waste can. Photo 3.29 also presents a negative inclusion issue. The "Main Entrance" is without access for many students.

Summary

In this chapter, numerous photographs were presented with my interpretation of how the photos could impact students. The more complex question is do students learn from these photographic messages of the hidden curriculum? In other words, are K-12 students impacted by these messages? Armstrong, Henson, and Savage (2001) answer this question in the affirmative: "Nearly all authorities

Photo 3.29 Physical Disability - Negative - Inclusion

agree that the hidden curriculum influences learner's attitudes toward the school program. There is a consensus that teachers need to be sensitive to all the messages that learners may be getting . . ." (p. 411). Photo 3.30 presents a visual answer to this question, as well. The photo is a rather large painting resulting from a class effort to meet the teacher's instructions to paint their "hometown." The

Photo 3.30 Painting of Hometown created by Students in Elementary School Class

hometown, in this case, has a river running through it. The students painted the river with several associated activities. The painting depicts the foregoing cell of Gender – Negative – Characteristics. The boys were painted fully engaged in activities with the river—swimming, boating, rafting, etc. Girls, on the other hand, were painted as spectators to the activity and engaged in childcare. The students had created a painting reflecting the hidden curriculum on characteristics associated with the binary of gender.

The aim of this chapter was to present how the artifacts of the hidden curriculum can send diversity messages, how to use a series of questions to help expose the hidden messages through interpretations, and how to move from individual photographs to salient themes. In the final chapter, the issues associated with the collection and utilization of school artifacts of the hidden curriculum are addressed.

References

Armstrong, D. G., Henson, K. T. & Savage, T. V. (2001). *Teaching today: An introduction to education.* 6th Edition. Upper Saddle River, N.J: Merrill Prentice Hall.

Banks, J. (2003). *An introduction to multicultural education.* 3rd ed. Boston: Allyn & Bacon.

Banning, J. H. (1988). Behavioral traces: A concept for campus ecologists. *The Campus Ecologist, 6*(2),1,3.

Banning, J. H. & Bartels, S. (1997). A taxonomy: Campus physical artifacts as communicators of campus multiculturalism. *NASPA Journal, 35*(1), 29-37.

Banning, J. H., Middleton, & Dennison, T. (2008). Using photographs to assess equity climate: A taxonomy. *Multicultural Perspectives, 10*(1), 41-46.

Banning, J. H., Sexton, J., Most, D. E., & Maier, S. (2007). Gender asymmetries encountered in the search and exploration of mining engineering program websites: A portrayal of posture and roles. *Journal of Women and Minorities in Science and Engineering, 13,*165-174.

Betz, N. E. (1989). Implications of the null environment hypothesis for women's career development and for counseling psychology. *The Counseling Psychologist, 17*(1), 136– 144.

Boyatzis, R. E. (1998). *Transforming qualitive information: Thematic analysis and code development.* Thousand Oaks, CA: Sage Publications.

Branaman, A. (Ed.). (2001). *Self and society.* New York: Blackwell Publishers.

Corbin, J., & Strauss, A. (2008). *Basics of qualitative research.* Los Angeles, CA: Sage.

Emmison, M., & Smith, P. (2000). Researching the visual. London: Sage Publications.

Freeman, J. (1979). How to discriminate against women without really trying. In J. Freeman(Ed.). *Women: A feminist perspective* (pp. 194–208). Palo Alto, CA: Mayfield.

Gagliardi,P. (Ed.). (1990). *Symbols and artifacts: Views of the corporate landscape.* New York: Adline de Gruyter.

King, N. (1998). Template analysis. In G. Symon & C. Cassell (Eds.). *Qualitative methods and analysis in organizational research:*

A practical guide (pp.118-134). Thousand Oaks, CA: Sage Publications.

Milgram, P., & Kishino, F. (1994). A taxonomy of mixed reality visual displays. *IEICE Transactions on Information Systems, E77-D* (12). Retrieved from http://vered.rose.utoronto.ca/people/paul_dir?IEIC94/ieice.html

Neuendorf, K. A. (2002). *The content analysis guidebook.* Thousand Oaks, CA: Sage Publications.

Pewewardy, C. D. (2000). Why educators should not ignore Indian mascots. *Multicultural Perspectives,* 2(1), 3-7.

Ragin, C. C. (2008). *Redesigning social inquiry: Fuzzy sets and beyond.* Chicago: Chicago University Press.

Strange, C. C., & Banning, J. H. (2015). *Designing for learning: Creating campus environments for student success.* San Francisco, CA: Jossey-Bass.

Zeisel, J. (1975). *Sociology and architectural design.* Russell Sage Social Science Frontiers Series, no 6. New York: Free Press.

Zeisel, J. (1981). *Inquiry by design:* Monterey, CA: Brooks/Cole.

Zeisel, J. (2006). *Inquiry by design: Environment/behavior/ neuroscience in architecture, interiors, landscape, and planning.* New York: W. W. Norton & Company.

COLLECTION AND UTILIZATION OF DIVERSITY PHOTOGRAPHS

In Chapter Three, the importance of the role of interpretation and the illustrations of diversity photographs were presented. To complete the purpose of this book, the collection and how to utilize the photographs in the examination and enhancement of school culture for diversity will be presented. Key to both the collection and utilization of diversity photographs is participation. Full participation of all school personnel is critical to both the collection and utilization. Many of the negative and problematic photos presented earlier in this chapter illustrate the problems when individuals and individual offices place artifacts in the school environment without meaningful discussion with diverse groups. For example, if a Native American group were to have been included in the choice of mascots, the offensive portrayals of Native Americans found in photos 3.22, 3.23, and 3.24 would have been unlikely to appear. Many of the gender-related posters would also have taken a different form if full participation included the women and students sensitive to gender issues. This broad participation from school constituencies is needed to address existing negative issues, to prevent new negative artifacts from appearing, and to support positive diversity artifacts in the classrooms and hallways of the school. The following strategies for collection and utilization of photographs all embrace the importance of participation.

Strategies for Collection and Participation

Solo Strategies

Solo strategies for the collection of photographs can take two forms: (1) Using an outside consultant, and (2) using a solo assessor from within the school. There are advantages and disadvantages to using an outside consultant. An outsider can bring a "fresh" set of eyes for observation and perhaps see and understand artifact messages that school personnel have become so accustomed to that they fail to see them. However, at the same time, the outsider does not have a full understanding of the school's history. To lessen this disadvantage, yet use the expertise and training of an outside consultant, the consulting role can move toward training. For example, local teachers and staff can be trained regarding how to recognize and interpret school artifacts relating to diversity. The trained individuals can then begin the collection of photographs for school discussion. The consultant's expertise is utilized, but the participation of the school is ensured through training and follow up within school discussions.

A second solo strategy is to recruit and designate individual teachers or staff members to collect photographs as they encounter the school environment in their daily routines. The individual photographs can be sent to a central depository site for collection and presentation for group discussion—again ensuring school participation and discussion. An important advantage of having individuals collect photographs during their normal activities at school is that they can initiate immediate action if they find disturbing artifacts. For example, a university class field trip to photograph a university library found that a considerable number of the book return carts had been vandalized with sexual graffiti. Photographs of the graffiti were not held for discussion, but immediate notification was made to the library staff. Currently, many K-12 schools have speedy graffiti removal policies. Having designated individuals taking photographs puts more "hands-on-deck" with critical information to start the removal process. (See Shade Box 4.1.) Photographs gathered by the solo photographers that raise questions regarding interpretation can be gathered for presentation and discussion at a variety of group gatherings, thereby, ensuring participation of the school.

Shade Box 4.1 Removal of School Artifacts

The school's artifacts that include hate messages and are presented in the form of graffiti should be removed immediately; however, historical school artifacts which send negative messages (statuary, murals, paintings, and monuments) and, in some manner, are "institutionalized," present a more complex decision process. Important ingredients to consider in the decision-making process regarding removal are the following:

- Most critical, the decision-making discussion process should include all school groups.

- Discussion should address the important issues regarding the ethics of social intervention (Kelman & Warwick, 1978) in addition to the full participation of the community.

  - Who will benefit and who will not benefit from the decision of removal?

  - What methods will be used to implement the decision of removal?

  - Who will monitor the process and outcomes of the removal?

- If the school retains an artifact that has a negative message for diversity, rather than removing it, the artifact needs to become transformational. Information regarding the artifact (history, purpose, importance, controversies, disagreements, etc.) needs to be placed near the artifact for public viewing and for inviting public thought and comment. The artifact becomes transformational in that it becomes an invitation for educational and personal thought. The placing of the issues of the artifact for public viewing and thought sends an important message that the school values community dialogue. It does not accept "White Silence" (DiAngelo, 2016), but, rather, it promotes open difficult discussions regarding matters of diversity.

Group Strategies

Schools can utilize many group strategies for the collection and utilization of diversity photographs, but two strategies will be highlighted: (1) teachers and staff can form groups to examine the school and gather photographs and (2) group projects that include students observing and collecting photographs. Using students in visual research to find meaning in the material culture is well supported (Thomson, 2008). Group observations highlight the simple procedure of designated school groups engaging in field trip like activities to gather photographs to present to various school groups and administrators for discussion and action, if necessary.

The second group strategy is open to creativity. For example, a graduate course in a student services in higher education program included the study of the campus environment. A project related to this curriculum goal was designed using the camera. Students were assigned different parking lots on campus to collect photographs of bumper stickers. The resulting photo collection was utilized for discussion to discover what cultural interests and values were being displayed. (See Shade Box 4.2.) K-12 schools could also employ a number of creative avenues. The bumper sticker project for the K-12 setting would have limited use, but with appropriate attention to privacy issues, student locker posters, notebook and computer stickers, and even student T-shirt messages could lead to important diversity discussions.

The solo and group strategies for the collection and utilization of diversity photographs are not restricted to the ones briefly discussed above. Many opportunities for creative processes exist, but critical to all strategies is the concept of full participation of school members.

Shade Box 4.2: Bumper Sticker Ethnography

Another Way to View the Campus Ecology

Ethnography

The focus of ethnographic inquiry is on answering the question: "What is the culture of this group of people?" (Patton, 1990). Traditionally, the method of choice was for the ethnographer to "live in" the culture as a participant observer and collect information about the culture through interviews, observations, and documents. Banning (1991) points out the usefulness of ethnographic approach in the attempt to understand the culture of the campus, and the notion of a campus cultural audit has been well documented (Kuh and Whitt, 1988; Whitt, 1993; Whitt and Kuh, 1991). Whitt (1993) defined a culture audit as providing "both insiders and outsiders with a means to systematically discover and identify the artifacts, values, and assumptions that comprise an organization's culture" (p. 83). Kuh and Whitt (1988) note that cultural assumptions and beliefs " . . . are just below the surface . . . manifested in observable forms or artifacts" (p. 16). Geertz (1973) suggests a similar notion that artifacts store cultural meaning. Banning and Bartels (1997) illustrate how photographs of cultural artifacts (artwork, posters, sculpture, physical structures, and graffiti) can help evaluate the multicultural "attitude" of a campus. The purpose of this article is to illustrate the potential of using "bumper stickers" as a campus cultural artifact to assist in the understanding of the campus culture or ecology.

Bumper Stickers

Carol Gardner (1995), in her book *Bumper Sticker Wisdom: America's Pulpit above the Tailpipe,* shares many important observations about bumper stickers. She notes that bumper stickers lead to a portrait of America: "...a nation of people in automobiles—that ultimate national icon—on the move with stickers expressing a view, sharing a frustration, or offering some perceived insight, solution, or wisdom" (p. 6). She goes on to note:

The bumper sticker may be an expression of personal philosophy, political anger and outrage, religious conviction, parental pride, sexual preference, or social comment. It may represent a simple statement of personal humor, ethnic identity, or class resentment. It may offer views of the opposite sex and marriage or of American culture and social institutions (p. 6).

Gardner (1995) also points out that "bumper stickers do not emerge in a vacuum but with the era and political culture of which they are a part" (p. 6). Can the aggregate of campus bumper stickers be another way to view the campus culture or ecology? The major themes of the culture suggested by the bumper stickers found on a college campus in the Rocky Mountain West are: (1) environmental issues and conflicts, (2) religious issues and conflicts, (3) sexual orientation issues, (4) political issues, (5) abortion issues, (6) violence issues, and (7) individualistic expressions.

Summary

Photographs can be taken to illustrate the potential of using campus bumper stickers as a way to understand campus culture. Several different approaches can be taken. The one illustrated in this article leads to a general view of the campus culture and is built on the notion of taking photographs of all the bumper stickers on campus — an aggregate view. A number of comparative approaches could also be implemented. For example, a comparison could be made between student bumper stickers and faculty bumper stickers. Perhaps generational differences might appear. Another possibility would be to compare stickers among student groups. How do the commuter parking lot bumper stickers compare to the ones in residence halls parking lots? Do stickers reflect academic majors? How do the stickers in the community parking lots (shopping malls, etc.) compare to the ones on campus? Many possibilities exist. Bumper sticker ethnography may not present the most refined picture of the campus ecology, but it is another way to view the campus culture—a fun way at that!

References

Banning, J. H. (1991). Ethnography: A promising method of inquiry for the study of campus ecology. *The Campus Ecologist, 9*(3), 1-3.

Banning, J. H. & Bartels, S. (1997). A taxonomy: Campus physical artifacts as communicators of campus multiculturalism. *NASPA Journal,* 35(1), 29-37. Washington. D. C.: National Association for Student Personnel Administrators.

Gardner, C. W. (I 995). *Bumper sticker wisdom: America's pulpit above the tailpipe.* Hillsboro, OR: Beyond Words Publishing Co.

Geertz, C. (l 973). *The interpretation of culture.* New York: Basic Books.

Kuh, G. D. & Whitt, E. J. (1988). The invisible tapestry: Cultures in American colleges and universities. *ASHE-ERIC Higher Education Report, No. 1.* Washington. D.C. Association for the Study of Higher Education.

Patton, M. (1990). *Qualitative evaluation and research methods.* Newbury Park, CA: Sage Publishing.

Whitt, E. J.(1993). Making the familiar strange: Discovering culture. In G. D. Kuh (Ed.). *Cultural perspectives in student affairs work* (pp.81-94). Washington, D.C. American College Personnel Association.

Whitt, E. J. & Kuh, G. D. (1991). The use of qualitative methods in a team approach to multiple institution studies. *The Review of Higher Education, 14,* 317-337.
Revised from the Campus Ecologist 1996.

Ethical Issues: Photographing School Artifacts

To leave the discussion of ethical issues to the closing of the manuscript does not suggest its lack of importance, but its juxtaposition to collection and utilization of photographs is important. Participation of others in all the aspects of photographing K-12 diversity messages is the critical ethical message, but there are also practical guidelines to be noted. See the chapter "On a pedagogy of ethics in visual research: Who's in the picture?" (Mitchell, C. M. (2011) for a very complete discussion of ethical issues. I use the following simple guidelines in my instructions to groups as they the collect and utilize photographs.

- Typically, the photographs should be of a physical aspect of a public place in the school environment and should not include people. The focus is on physical artifacts.

- If the desired photograph is in private spaces (offices, for example), then permission to photograph must be obtained from the "owner" of the space. The owner should be given an opportunity to view the photograph and information as to how the photograph will be used prior to giving consent.

- If the desired photograph includes people, permission from the persons must be obtained, the resulting photograph must be reviewed by the persons, and an explanation be given to the participating people regarding how it is to be used.

- School privacy policies should be reviewed and followed.

• Remember that no photograph is worth the invasion of someone's privacy.

Summary

The purpose of this book was to present a practical approach to how to photograph diversity messages found in school artifacts that expose the hidden curriculum on diversity. The notions of hidden curriculum, non-verbal communication, and visual/photographic research provided the connection to key conceptual and research efforts that are supportive of this very practical endeavor of photographing the K-12 diversity messages within the hidden curriculum. Tools of interpretation were provided to assist in discovering the possible diversity messages attached to the school artifacts found in the classrooms and hallways.

On a final note, social justice must be the foundation of the educational enterprise, and our schools' artifacts must include the celebration and social action needed so that all students can fully participate in school and society's activities. To help ensure these conditions, we must understand the diversity messages of school artifacts. We can photograph, interpret, and change these messages—enhancing the positive and changing the negative. Teachers have not only a special responsibility in bringing about a more inclusive environment, but a great opportunity to do so. Previna (2011) noted that "In a political era where teachers are given less and less autonomy over the school's official curriculum, the classroom is one of the few places where teachers are still granted a modicum of independence and the discretion to exercise agency" (p. v). The aim of this practical approach to exposing hidden curriculum regarding K-12 diversity is to give teachers and school personnel the understanding as to how to use the camera to improve their schools and contribute to the historical relationship between photography and social justice.

References

DiAngelo, R. (2016). *What does it mean to be white? Developing white racial literacy* New York: W. W. Norton & Co.

Kelman, H., & Warwick, D. (1978). The ethics of social intervention: Goals, means consequences. In G. Bemant, H. Kelman, & D. Warwick (Eds.). *The ethics of social intervention* (pp.3-33). New York: Wiley and Sons.

Mitchell, C. (2011). *Doing visual research.* Los Angeles: Sage Publications.

Previma, D. S. (2011). *Hidden in plain view: Classroom space, teacher agency, and the hidden curricula* (Doctoral Dissertation). Retrieved from the ProQuest Dissertation and Theses Global Database. (UMI No. 3486009).

Thomson, P. 2008 (Ed.). *Doing visual research with children and young people.* New York: Routledge.

APPENDIX A

Appendix A includes Chapter One from the book *Campus Artifacts as Diversity Messages: A Photographic Approach.* It is reprinted here for those who wish to look at the basic concepts critical to the understanding of photographing the school artifacts of the hidden curriculum.

LINES OF SCHOLARSHIP

The Ecological Perspective, Material Culture, and Visual/Photographic Observations

During my supervision of doctoral dissertations, I often used a Western culture "social greeting" analogy to help students to sort out their review of literature efforts. Some literature finds should be treated like greeting an acquaintance from afar—you wave. Other literature should be treated like meeting a casual friend on the street—you say hello, shake hands, and have a short conversation. Finally, however you greet a very close friend—you hug! Literature finds should be treated in a similar manner: some you wave to, some you say hello to, and a few you will want to hug closely.

The intention of this book is to provide very practical ways to read and interpret the material culture of the campus setting. It is unwise to be practical, however, without at least noting some background scholarship for the practical efforts. Practice without theory is risky. The foundational scholarship topics include the ecological perspective, material culture, and visual/photographic research, and these topics will be viewed as scholarship "lines" (Ingold, 2015). There is not enough time and space in this book to give these topics a "hug," but they deserve more than a "wave." So, I will address each of the concepts with important literature citations and provide resource references and resource illustrations in sections noted as a shaded box. These efforts will serve as the "hello" and a door to the "hug." First, however, more about scholarship lines.

Scholarship Lines

To organize the conceptual and literature background that supports the use of photographs to capture the messages of material culture, three conceptual/scholarship areas are important: an ecological perspective, understanding material culture, and visual/photographic research. I first thought of these three areas as the conceptual building blocks that support the purpose of this book, but after being exposed to the work of Ingold (2007, 2015, & 2016) and Hodder (2012) I think "lines" is a more useful terminology than "building blocks."

Ingold uses the concept of lines to explore anthropology and then suggests that the concept of lines promotes thinking about how lines become "entangled" together (Hodder, 2012) to form knots. These entangled lines eventually form surfaces that are referred to by Ingold (2015, p.83) as "meshwork." What I am suggesting is that we look at the lines of scholarship representing the ecological perspective, material culture, and visual/photographic research to form the entanglement or the surface for supporting the importance of understanding the cultural messages of a campus's material culture and capturing these messages in photographs. Of significance to campus life and the focus of this manuscript are the messages surrounding the notion of diversity.

These three lines of scholarship are not crisp sets or parallel lines but rather a fuzzy intersection. I first introduce the three lines of scholarship and then suggest in chapter two that Rapoport's (1982) nonverbal communication approach to material culture provides the "meshwork" for understanding how the ecological perspective, material culture, and visual/photographic research come together or "tangle" to give a practical approach to understanding campus culture. The notion of material culture playing a significant role in communicating culture is not new (Kuh, 1993; Kuh & Whitt, 1988;

Whitt, 1993). Kuh and Whitt and their colleagues can provide an important "hug" for understanding campus culture.

The Ecological Perspective Line

As I noted in a recent publication (Banning, 2016), the ecological perspective's scholarship line is long and rich and impossible to cover in just a few pages. Etymology is a place to start. The word ecology stems from the Greeks and means the "study of the house" (Kormonday & Brown, 1998). Later, the word was involved in denoting the interaction of animals and their environment. Ecology was later in the mid-nineteenth century defined within the scientific community by Ernst Haeckel for use in the study of evolution (Kormonday & Brown, 1998). The next major movement was the establishment of the field of human ecology. It is the field of human ecology that serves as the immediate backdrop for the scholarship line for viewing the campus environment as an important issue to campus culture. Human ecology is defined as the study of the relationships between people and their environment (Marten, 2001). Campus ecology (Banning, 2016) takes the concept of human behavior in relation to the natural, social, and built environments and focuses on the college and university campus. For example, Banning and Kuk (2005) defined the concept of campus ecology as follows:

> The concept of campus ecology is defined as the study of the campus as an ecological system made up of three components. The first is the organism/inhabitant component which includes students, faculty, staff, visitors, and others associated with the campus. The second component is the settings/environments component, and it includes both the social environment (the curriculum, the co-curriculum, the extra-curricular, and other social functions) and the physical environment (buildings, landscapes, walkways, and other natural and constructed features of the environment). The third component is the activities/behaviors component (learning, research, personal development, and other outcomes specific to higher education). (p. xx)

In summary, the scholarship line of the ecological perspective underscores the importance of studying "campus as house" and the artifacts within that make up the material culture of the campus.

Shade Box Appendix A-1: Resource References for the Ecological Perspective

Amedo, D., Golledge, R., & Stimson, R. (2009). *Person environment behavior research*. New York: The Guildford Press.

Banning, J. H. (Ed.). (1978). *Campus ecology: A perspective for student affairs*. Cincinnati, OH: NASPA Monograph.

Banning, J. H. (2016). *Campus ecology and university affairs: History, Applications, and Future*. Arvada, CO: TerraCotta Publishing.

Banning, J. H.,& Kaiser, L. (1974). Ecological perspective and model for campus design. *The Personnel and Guidance Journal, 52*(6), 370-375.

Barker, R. G. (1968*). Ecological psychology: Concepts and methods for studying the environment of human behavior*. Stanford, CA: Stanford University Press.

Bronfenbrenner, U. (1979). *The ecology of human development: Experiments by nature and design*. Cambridge, MA: Harvard University Press.

Brunswik, E. (1956). *Perception and the representative design of psychological experiments*. Berkeley, CA: University of California Press.

Conyne, R. K., & Clack, R. J. (1981). *Environmental assessment and design*. New York: Praeger Publishers.

Heft, H. (2001). *Ecological psychology in context*. New York: Psychology Press.

Kelly, J. G. (2006). *Becoming ecological: An expedition into community psychology.* New York: Oxford University Press.

Kemp, S., Whittaker, J., & Tracy, E. (1997). *Person-environment practice: The social ecology of*

interpersonal helping. New York: Adline De Gruyter.

Kormonday, E. J., & Brown, D. E. (1998). *Fundamentals of Human Ecology.* Upper Saddle River, NJ: Prentice-Hall.

Lewin, K. (1936). *Principles of topological psychology.* New York: McGraw Hill.

Michael, W. B., & Boyer, E. L. (1965). Campus environment. *Review of Educational Research, 35*(4), 264-276.

Stern, G. G. (1965). Student ecology and the college environment. *Journal of Medical Education, 40,* 132-54.

Strange, C. C., & Banning, J. H. (2001). *Educating by design: Creating campus environments That work.* San Francisco, CA: Jossey-Bass.

Strange, C. C., & Banning, J. H. (2015). *Designing for learning: Creating campus environments for student success.* San Francisco, CA: Jossey-Bass.

Walsh, W. B. (1973). Theories of person-environment interaction: Implications for the college student. Iowa City, IA: American College Testing Program.

Walsh, W. B. (1978). Person/Environment Interaction. In J. H. Banning (Ed). *Campus ecology: A Perspective for Student Affairs* (pp. 6-16). Cincinnati, OH: National Student Personnel.

The Material Culture Line

The concept of material culture falls within several disciplines, and its definition has loose boundaries. Berger (2014) refers to material culture as the "world of things that people make" (p. 16). "Stuff" is the concept used by Miller (2010, p. 1). For the purposes of this manuscript, Prown's (1982) definition is helpful: "The term *material culture* ... refers quite directly and efficiently, if not elegantly, both to the subject matter of the study, *material*, and to its purpose, the understanding of *culture*" (p. 2). Berger (2014) best describes and summarizes the scholarship line of material culture:

> Cultural values and beliefs take form or are manifested in artifacts and objects—that is, in material culture. What this suggests is that we can use artifacts to help us gain insights into the culture that produced them, if we know how to interpret or "read" them. Material culture gives us a means of understanding better the societies and cultures that produce the objects and use them." (p. 17)

The material culture line of scholarship provides the conceptual support to the key notion of this manuscript that campus artifacts contain messages (encoded) by the campus culture and that these messages can be read (decoded) by inhabitants and visitors to the campus. Campus messages regarding diversity are a prime example of this encoding and decoding process. The purpose of this book is further supported by Berger (2014) when he notes: "Generally speaking, we can say that if you can photograph it and it isn't too large, we can consider it to be an example of material culture" (p. 17). The next section of this introductory chapter presents the third scholarship line: Visual/Photographic Research.

Shade Box Appendix A-2: Resource References for Material Culture

Berger, A. (2014). *What objects mean: An introduction to material culture.* (2nd Edition). Walnut Creek, CA: Left Costal Press.

Csikszentmihalyi, M., & Rochberg-Halton, E. (1981). *The meaning of things: Domestic symbols and the self.* Cambridge, UK: Cambridge University Press.

Deely, J. (1982). *Introducing semiotics: Its history and doctrine.* Bloomington: Indiana University Press.

Frutiger, A. (1989). *Signs and symbols.* New York: Van Nostrand Reinhold.

Geertz, C. (1973). *The interpretation of cultures.* New York: Basic Books.

Hodder, I. (2012). *Entangled: An Archaeology of the relationships between humans and things.* West Sussex, UK: Wiley-Blackwell Publishers.

Hodge, R., & Kress, G. (1988). *Social semiotics.* Ithaca, NY: Cornell University Press.

Ingold, T. (2015). *The life of lines.* London: Routledge Classics.

Ingold, T. (2016). *Lines.* New York: Routledge Classics.

Lubar, S., & Kingery, W. D. (1993). *History of things: Essays on material culture.* Washington, D.C.: Smithsonian Institution.

Miller, D. (2010). *Stuff.* Malden, MA: Polity.

Money, A. (2007). *Material culture and the living room. Journal of Consumer Culture, 7*(3), 355-377.

Myers, F. R. (2002). *The empire of things: Regimes of value and material culture.* Santa Fe, NM: School of American Research Press.

Prown, J. D. (1982). Mind in matter: An introduction to material culture theory and method. *Winterthur Portfolio, 17*(1), 1-19.

Sebeok, T. (1986). (Ed.) *Encyclopedia dictionary of semiotics.* New York: Mouton de Gruyter.

Sless, D. (1986). *In search of semiotics.* Totowa, NJ: Barnes and Nobel Books.

Tilley, C. (1999). *Metaphor and material culture.* Oxford, UK: Blackwell Publishers.

Tilley, C., Keane, W., Kuchler, S., Rowlands, M., & Spyer, P. (Eds.). (2006). *Handbook of material culture.* London: Sage Publications.

Architectural Readings

Bonta, J. (1979). *Architecture and its interpretation: A study of expressive systems in architecture.* London: Lund Humphries.

Preziosi, D. (1979). *The semiotics of the built environment: An introduction to architectonic analysis.* Bloomington: Indiana University Press.

Rapoport, A. (1982). *The meaning of the built environment.* Beverly Hills, CA: Sage Publications.

Clarke, D. S. (1987). *Principles of semiotics.* New York: Routledge & Kegan.

Visual/Photographic Research Line

Observational methods fall into two categories: obtrusive and unobtrusive (Webb, Campbell, Schwartz, & Sechrest, 1996). The obtrusive methods involve the observer being placed directly into the phenomena of interest and the presence of the observer influencing the observation. Unobtrusive methods gather observational data but without direct involvement with the people of interest. The unobtrusive is also referred to as non-reactive observation (Lee, 2000). An example important to this manuscript is the use of photographs (Emmison & Smith, 2000) to capture the meaning of campus cultural artifacts. This method places emphasis on the visual rather than the verbal.

Sanoff (1991) stated that much of historical environmental research has "relied on verbal descriptions and perceptions of the physical environment, virtually ignoring the importance of the visual component" (p. ix). Willig (2011) makes a similar observation: "(There is a) ... noticeable lack of accommodation of the 'visual' in contemporary qualitative psychology ... (it can) enrich our understanding of meaning-making and experience ... can add to our understanding of the human experience" (p.xxv). Rose (2007) notes the importance of the visual image in understanding "how social life happens" (p. xii). Reavey (2011) underlines cultural connection to the visual by noting that the "visual is an integral part of the way in which culture operates (p. xxvi). The connection of the visual to the cultural is similarly endorsed by Prosser (1998), when he states that the visual is a "significant manifestation of culture" (p. 2). The advantages of the visual approach are outlined by Spencer (2011). He notes that the visual is immediate and explicit, that it can help to create narratives, and that it provides "a 'thick description' that helps in exploring and finding meaning" (p. 33).

Key to this supporting line of visual scholarship is the link between the visual as observation to using photographs to capture the meaning of the visual. Raggel and Shratz (2004) pointing to the visual and the use of photographs state: "... (photographs) demonstrated how social life is frequently situated, shaped, and given social significance by the interaction of individuals, with artifacts and spaces" (p. 7). As will be highlighted in chapter two of this manuscript, the link between artifacts in the campus environment and the interpretation of photographs of those artifacts is complex. The adage that "pictures don't lie" fails to capture the complexity of the interpretative process going from the photograph to its meaning, even the complexity of which artifacts are chosen to be photographed. Ball (1998) makes this point very clear: "As a form of data, photographs are not capable of talking for themselves, the information has to be teased out of them, interpreted and decoded, the visual availability of the phenomena has to be unpacked" (p. 137). Byers (1966) gives a succinct summary: "cameras don't take pictures, people do" (p. 27). My role as the photographer/interpreter regarding diversity will be addressed in chapter three.

Shade Box Appendix A-3: Resource References for Visual/ Photographic Research

Visual References: General

Ball, M. S., & Smith, G. W. H. (1992). *Analyzing visual data* (Qualitative Research Methods Series, Vol. 24). Newbury Park, CA Sage.

Banks, M. (2007). *Using visual data in qualitative research*. Los Angeles: Sage Publication.

Banks, M., & Morphy, H. (Eds.). (1997). *Rethinking visual anthropology*. New Haven, CT: Yale University Press.

Barthes, R. (1996). *Camera Lucida: Reflections on Photography*. New York: Hill and Wang.

Bauer, M. W. & Gaskell, G. (Eds.) (2000). *Qualitative researching with text, image, and sound*. London: Sage.

Becker, H. S. (1978). Do photographs tell the truth? *After Image, 5,* 9-13.

Becker, H. S. (1986). *Doing things together: Selected papers*. Evanston, IL: Northwestern Press.

Collier, J. J., & Collier, M. (1986). *Visual anthropology: Photography as a research method*. Albuquerque, NM: University of New Mexico Press.

Dabbs, J. M. (1982). Making things visible. In J. Van Maanen, J. M. Dabbs, & R. Faulkner, (Eds.). *Varieties of Qualitative Research* (pp. 31-64). London: Sage.

Denzin, N. K. (1989). *The research act* (3rd ed.) Englewood Cliffs, NJ: Prentice-Hall.

Emmison, M., & Smith, P. (2000). *Researching the visual.* London: Sage Publications.

Graeme, S. (2005). *Art practice as research. Inquiry in the visual arts.* Thousand Oaks, CA: Sage.

Harper, D. (1989). Visual Sociology: Expanding sociological vision. In G. Bank, J. L. McCartney and E. Brent. (Eds.). *New Technologies in sociology: Practical application in research and work* (pp. 81-97). New Brunswick, NJ: Transaction Books.

Harper, D. (1994). On the authority of the image: Visual Methods at the crossroads. In N. Denzin, & Y. S. Lincoln, (Eds.). *Handbook of Qualitative Research* (pp.403-12). London, Sage.

Hesse-Biber, S. N., & Leavy, P. (Eds.). (2008). *Handbook of emergent methods.* New York: Guilford Press.

Hockings, P. (Ed.) (1995). *Principles of visual anthropology.* (2nd Edition) Berlin: Mouton de   Gruyter.

Knowles, J. G., & Cole, A. L. (Eds.). (2008). *Handbook of the arts in qualitative research.* Los Angeles: Sage.

Pink, S. (2001). *Doing visual ethnography.* London: Sage Publications.

Pole, C. (Ed.). (2004). *Seeing is believing? Approaches to visual research.* London: Elsevier.

Prosser, J. (Ed.). (1998). *Image-based research: A sourcebook for qualitative researchers.* London: Falmer Press.

Rose, G. (2007). *Visual methodologies: An introduction to the interpretation of visual materials.* (2nd ed.). Los Angeles: Sage Publications.

Smith, K., Moriarty, S., Barbatsis, G., & Kenney, K. (Eds). (2005). *Handbook of visual communication: Theory, methods, and media*. Mahwah, NJ: Lawrence Erlbaum Assoc. Publishers.

Stanczak, G. C. (Ed.). (2007). *Visual research methods: Image, society, and representation*. Los Angeles: Sage.

Sturken, M., & Cartwright, L. (2001). *Practice of looking: An introduction to visual culture*. Oxford, NY: Oxford Press.

Templin, P. A. (1982). Still photography in evaluation. In N. L. Smith (Ed.). *Communication strategies in evaluation*. (pp. 121-175). Beverly Hills, CA: Sage.

Thomson, P. (Ed). (2008). *Doing visual research with children and young people*. London: Routledge.

Van Leeuwen, T., & Jewitt, C. (2001). *Handbook of visual analysis*. London: Sage Publications.

Wagner, J. (Ed.). (1979). *Images of information*. Beverly Hills, CA: Sage.

Wang, C., & Burris, M. A. (1997). Photovoice: Concept, methodology, and use for participatory needs assessment. *Health education & behavior, 24*(3), 369-387.

Wang, C. C., Yi, W. K., Tao, Z. W., & Carovano, K. (1998). Photovoice as a participatory health promotion strategy. *Health promotion international, 13*(1), 75-86.

Visual References: Personal/Applied Work

Banning, J. H. (1992). Visual anthropology: Viewing the campus ecology for messages of sexism. *The Campus Ecologist, 10*(1), 1-4.

Banning, J. H. (1995). Campus images: Homoprejudice. *The Campus Ecologist, 12*(3), 3.

Banning, J. H. (1997). Assessing the Campus' Ethical Climate: A Multidimensional approach. In J. Fried, (Ed). *Ethics for today's Campus: New Perspectives on education, student development, and institutional management* (pp. 95-105). (New Direction for Student Services #77), San Francisco: Jossey-Bass Publishers.

Banning, J. H., & Bartels, S. (1997). A taxonomy: Campus physical artifacts as communicators of Campus multiculturalism. *NASPA Journal, 35*(1), 29-37.

Banning, J. H., & McKelfresh, D. A. (1998). Using photographs of the housing mission statement in staff training. *Talking Stick, 15*(8), 22-24.

Banning, J. H., Middleton, V., & Deniston, T. L. (2008). Using photographs to assess equity climate: A taxonomy. *Multicultural Perspectives, 10*(1), 41-46.

Banning, J. H., & Luna, F. C. (1992). Viewing the campus ecology for messages about Hispanic/Latino culture. *The Campus Ecologist 10* (4), 1-4.

Banning, J. H., Sexton, J., Most, D. E. & Maier, S. (2007). Gender asymmetries encountered in the search and exploration of mining engineering program websites: A portrayal of posture and roles. *Journal of Women and Minorities in Science and Engineering 13*, 165-176.

Kaminski, K., & Banning, J. (2007) Visuals in public places: Whose interpretation is it? In R. E. Griffin, M. D. Averinou, & J. Gieson (Eds.). *History, community, and culture: Celebrating tradition and transforming the future* (pp.109-114). Indianapolis, IN: IDEC.

Marley, J., Nobe, M. C., Clevenger, C. M. & Banning, J. H. (2015). Participatory post-occupancy evaluation (PPOE): A method to include students in evaluating health-promoting attributes of a green school. *Children, Youth, and Environments, 25*(1), 4-28.

Sexton, J. M., O'Connell, S., Banning, J. H., & Most, D. (2014). Characteristics and culture of geoscience departments as interpreted from their website photographs. *Journal of Women and Minorities in Science and Engineering, 20*(93), 257-278.

The Campus Ecologist articles are available at http://www. campusecologist.com

Summary

In summary, the ecological perspective highlights the focus on the environment as a significant factor in determining behavior and examining culture. Within the environment resides the material culture of the built environment and adornments that provide opportunity for photographing and interpreting the cultural messages. The elements/ objects of the material culture can be observed and photographed for discussion and evaluation, and, if needed, they can be changed.

In chapter two, I introduce Rapoport's (1982) nonverbal communication approach to material culture as providing the "meshwork" for understanding how the ecological perspective, material culture, and visual/photographic research come together in a "tangle" or "knot" to give a practical approach to understanding campus culture.

References

Ball, M. (1998). Remarks on visual competence as an integral part of ethnographic fieldwork practice: The visual availability of culture. In J. Prosser, (Ed.). *Image-based research: A sourcebook for qualitative researchers* (pp.131-147). London: Falmer Press.

Banning, J. H. (2016). *Campus ecology and university affairs: History, applications, and future.* Arvada, CO: TerraCotta Publishing.

Banning, J. H., & Kuk, L. (2005). Campus ecology and college student health. *Spectrum,* November 9-15.

Berger, A. (2014). *What objects mean: An introduction to material culture.* (2nd Edition). Walnut Creek, CA: Left Costal Press.

Byers, P. (1966). "Cameras don't take pictures." *Columbia University Forum, 9,* 27-31. Emmison, M., & Smith, P. (2000). *Researching the visual.* London: Sage Publications.

Hodder, I. (2012). *Entangled: An Archaeology of the relationships between humans and things.* West Sussex, UK: Wiley-Blackwell Publishers.

Ingold, T. (2007). *Lines: A brief history.* Abingdon, UK: Routledge.

Ingold, T. (2015). *The life of lines.* London: Routledge Classics.

Ingold, T. (2016). *Lines.* New York: Routledge Classics.

Kormonday, E. J., & Brown, D. E. (1998). *Fundamentals of Human Ecology.* Upper SaddleRiver, NJ: Prentice-Hall.

Kuh, G. D. (Ed.). (1993). *Cultural perspectives in student affairs work.* Washington, D.C. American College PersonnelAssociation.

Kuh, G. D., & Whitt, E. J. (1988). The invisible tapestry: Cultures in American colleges and universities. ASHE-ERIC Higher Education Report, No. 1. Washington, C. Association for the Study of Higher Education.

Lee, R. M. (2000). *Unobtrusive methods in social research.* Buckingham, UK: Open University Press.

Marten, G. G. (2001). *Human ecology: Basic concepts for sustainable development.* Sterling, VA: Earthscan Publications Ltd.

Miller, D. (2010). *Stuff.* Cambridge, UK: Polity Press.

Prosser, J. (Ed.). (1988). Introduction. In J. Prosser, (Ed.). *Image-based research: A sourcebook for qualitative researchers* (pp. 1-5). London: Falmer Press.

Prown, J. D. (1982). Mind in matter: An introduction to material culture theory and method. *Winterthur Portfolio, 17*(1), 1-19.

Raggel, A., & Shratz, M. (2004). Using visuals to release pupil's voices: Emotional pathways into enhancing thinking and reflecting on learning. In C. Pole (Ed.). *Seeing is believing? Approaches to visual research* (pp. 147-181). Amsterdam, NL: Elsevier.

Rapoport, A. (1982). *The meaning of the built environment: A nonverbal communications approach.* Beverly Hills, CA: Sage Publications.

Reavey, P. (Ed.) (2011). *Visual methods in psychology: Using and interpreting images in qualitative research.* New York: Psychology Press.

Rose, G. (2007). *Visual methodologies: An introduction to the interpretation of visual materials.* (2nd ed.). Los Angeles: Sage Publications

Spencer, S. (2011). *Visual research methods in the social sciences: Awakening visions.* London: Routledge.

Sanoff, H. (1991). *Visual research methods in design.* New York: Van Nostrand Reinhold.

Webb, E. J., Campbell, D. T., Schwartz, R. D., & Sechrest. L. (1996). *Unobtrusive measures: Nonreactive research in the social sciences.* Chicago, IL: Rand McNally.

Whitt, E. J. (1993). Making the familiar strange: Discovering culture. In G. D. Kuh (Ed.). *Cultural perspectives in student affairs work* (pp.81-94). Washington, D.C. American College PersonnelAssociation.

Willig, C. (2011). Forward. In P. Reavey (Ed.) *Visual methods in psychology: Using and interpreting images inqualitative research.* (p. xxv). New York: Psychology Press.

APPENDIX B

Appendix B is a compilation and editing of several articles previously published in *The Campus Ecologist* (http://www. campusecologist.com). Photographs have been added to illustrate the use of the behavioral/physical trace approach.

Material Culture, Behavior, and the Physical Trace Approach to Assessment

Discussion of the topic of behavior and the built material environment often starts by referring to the Winston Churchill statement that we shape our buildings and then they shape us. This observation leads to the question of what role material culture plays in student behavior. This question can be pursued from an ecological perspective by looking at the major issue embedded in the architecture/building and behavior relationship.

Nature of Influence

The major issue that needs to be addressed is the nature of the influence that material culture in general and buildings in specific may have on behavior. In the literature, the nature of this influence has been conceptualized by three positions (Bell, Fisher, Baum, & Greene, 1990; Porteus, 1977). First, *architectural determinism* suggests that there is a rather direct and causal link between the built environment and behavior. A second position, environmental *or architectural possibilism* views the building as one that offers opportunities and sets limits for behavior. This relationship is denoted by context rather than determinism. Finally, environmental or *architectural probabilism* assumes that certain behaviors have probabilistic links to the built environment.

While all three positions offer insight into the relationship between material culture and behavior, to assume the position of architectural determinism suggests buildings have a direct and causal link to behavior. This position, however, does not do justice to the complexities of the environment, the complexities of behavior, nor the diversity of the students. It fails to capture the transactional relationship between buildings, students, and behavior; that is, it fails to sort out the complex social and psychological factors associated with built spaces (Porteus, 1977).

To view the relationship in terms of possibilities and probabilities, however, not only appears more realistic, it also captures our intuitive notion that campus buildings can make a difference in the lives of students.

What are the important behaviors that can be influenced by the architecture of the building? Deasy and Lasswell (1985), an architect and sociologist, respectively, outline eight behavioral categories that can be influenced by architecture. These categories have direct application to the campus environment. Deasy and Lasswell list these as follows: (1) friendship formation, (2) group membership, (3) personal space, (4) personal status, (5) territoriality, (6) communications, (7) cue searching, and (8) personal safety.

In other words, the architecture can make possible and increase probability of friendship and group involvement by designing spaces that bring people together. Personal needs of privacy and personalization can also be impacted by the architecture. Students, like all of us, seek private and personal spaces they can retreat to and call their own. Some spaces facilitate communication among students, and other space arrangements often hinder important communications. Classrooms can often be seen from this framework. Cue-searching or way-finding is the notion that the architecture can help us navigate the campus. The architecture can either confuse us or guide us. Finally, architecture of "doors" can either increase or decrease the probability of being safe.

Given the influence that architecture has on important student behaviors, Deasy and Lasswell's suggestion that all building/program plans of new construction or renovations should carry what they call "behavioral program" makes for good student affairs practice. Seeking out all messages related to campus material culture is likewise good student affairs practice.

Campus behavioral programs related to architecture and other elements of the material culture need not be a mystery. These behaviors can be detected by keen observation using nonverbal cues for the assessment or appraisal of the material artifacts.

This observational process can be used to gather information to assist in the diagnostic efforts as well as the selection of possible intervention strategies regarding organizational issues, such as campus diversity. What, then, are the conceptual tools that can lead to greater understanding of organizations and campus environments through the examination of the material culture?

Physical Traces: A Conceptual Tool for Understanding the Organization

It is important to note that buildings and organizations have important direct functional relationships. For example, is there enough space to carry out the functions of the organization? The physical environment not only affords certain activities and constrains others in a functional sense (Wohlwill, & Heft, 1989), but these functional arrangements of affordances and constraints also communicate non-verbal messages (Weinstein & David, 1987). How can we increase our understanding of organizations by attending to the non-verbal messages of the organization's physical environment (Rapoport, 1982)? One of the more useful strategies is to view the organization's physical environment from a behavioral traces perspective (Zeisel, 1981), including the symbolic messages accompanying the behavioral trace (Rapoport, 1982; Steele, 1973).

As organizational activities interact with physical spaces, the behavior leaves "traces" (Bechtel & Zeisel, 1987). These behavioral traces can be interpreted as non-verbal messages that increase the understanding of campus behavior (Banning, 1988). As Bechtel and Zeisel state: "Few give a thought ... to the fact that the fossils of tomorrow are the garbage dumps of today" (1987, p. 32). Zeisel (1981) presents a number of ways "to read" traces that can be useful in gaining a fuller understanding of organizational environments. Zeisel's methods are: (1) by-products of use, (2) adaptation of use, (3) displays of self, and (4) public messages.

By-products of Use

Photo A1 Erosion   *Photo A2 Eroded Chair Arms*

By-products are produced by people interacting with the environment. These by-products of behavior can be further defined by the concepts of erosion, leftovers, missing traces, and accretions (Bechtel and Zeisel, 1987). A simple example of *erosion* on campus is the worn paths (shown in Photo A1) that students make as they find the shortest distance between campus buildings. Worn furniture in an admissions office waiting area is another example of erosion that has greater negative impact on institutional image. Worn or eroded armchairs suggest fiddling or nervousness (Photo A2). These are not the physical traces that suggest a comfortable admissions office visit.

Leftovers are traces represented by objects not consumed in the behavior. Trash and litter are the most common examples. Leftovers can also become associated with campus issues. For example, Photo A3 illustrates that students are unwilling to place recyclable items in a trash receptacle, and these leftovers are accumulating at the top. The issue could be resolved by adding a recycle bin for plastics. Another

Photo A3 Trash Receptacle

example of leftovers can be found in Photo A4: Restroom. As a part of a task to view residence halls' material culture

Photo A4 Restroom

in relation to their mission statement (Banning & McKelfresh, 1998), the restroom photo was taken to illustrate the need to be more diligent and timely in the cleaning of restrooms. This restroom was designated for visitors to the residence hall, and the leftovers do not send a very positive public message.

Bechtel and Zeisel (1987) use the concept of *missing traces* to

Photo A5 Bike Rack

indicate a lack of use in areas where erosion and leftovers are expected but do not show up. Many campus spaces have been designed in such a manner as to ensure that they will never be used by people on campus. The documentation of this lack of use or "missing traces" is often helpful in gaining support for a redesign of the space to better serve the needs of the campus. For example, Photo A5 shows a bike rack unused despite heavy bicycle traffic on campus due to its location (not being near an entrance to the building). For better use, the bike rack needs to be moved closer to an entrance. Finally, the concept of *accretion* is used to denote the buildup of materials on physical objects. For example, dust on books in the library that have not been checked out or buildup of fingerprints on frequently used doorknobs.

Adaptation for Use

Zeisel (1981) uses the concept of adaptation for use to encompass situations in the environment where a change has been made because the first design did not serve its original intention. The physical environment is changed to better accommodate campus behavior. These adaptations or accommodations are classified by Zeisel (1981) as props, separations, and connections.

Campus adaptation for use would include renovations, expansions, and other changes or improvements. Often the attempt by students to "adapt" a space for an unintended purpose is the first cue that a redesign effort may be needed. Props are items that are added to or moved from a setting. For example, chairs (props) are often moved around in a building by students to better accommodate their seating patterns. By following the adding, moving, and removing of props from a setting, insights can be gained regarding inhabitant behavior. Photo A6 suggests that sitting for traditional telephone behavior is more desirable than standing.

Separations are those changes in which the inhabitants of the physical space separate spaces formerly together to achieve some

Photo A6 Telephone Seat

Photo A7 Roomate Seperation

behavioral outcomes. The creativity displayed by students in developing separations in the traditional residence hall room to achieve privacy and a sense of territory is a clear example.

Connections are physical adaptations that connect settings allowing for different behaviors. On one campus, a makeshift sidewalk appeared in order to connect the rear parking lot to the main entrance to a new student center. The need for this connection was due to the failure of the original design to place a rear entrance to the building. Physical connections can also produce symbolic connections. On one campus, a bridge was built to link two parts of a campus that had been separated by an irrigation ditch. The bridge, however, took on symbolic meaning when it was constructed in part from the bricks off "old main" that burned down during a Vietnam-era protest. The bridge was designed by a group of veterans as well as a group of protesters to the war and dedicated to bridge or "connect" the differing points of view toward the war.

Displays of Self

Zeisel (1981) uses the concept of "display of self" to illustrate how the material cultural can be used to convey messages about individual and group ownership. Three categories represent this concept:

Personalization or the use of the physical environment to express uniqueness and individuality. Resident doors with adornments within a residence hall is an example.

Photo A8 Oil Derrick

Identification or the use of the physical environment to enable others to identify the function of the environment. For example, on one campus there is a small "oil derrick" atop the petroleum engineering building (Photo A8).

Group membership or the use the physical environment to

Photo A9 Fraternity House

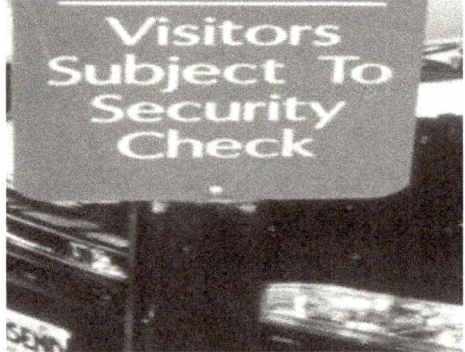

Photo A10 Welcome Sign

display membership in formal groups and organizations. The Greek letters on fraternity and sorority houses are a clear example. The "letter" display can also send non-verbal messages about organizational values. Fraternity houses that display artifacts of their activities send a clear message regarding house values. For example, the fraternity house in Photo 9A shows a disrespect for the American flag, a flying of the Confederate flag, and a "borrowed" Taco Bell advertisement banner.

Public Messages

The last category for Zeisel is public messages. Included in this concept are traces that range from official signs, unofficial signs and symbols, and graffiti. *Official signs* are erected by officials of the environment or organization. Often, however, these signs contain non-intended messages. For example, a welcome sign to visitors that also includes a warning that they may be searched while on campus is less than welcoming (Photo A10). *Unofficial signs* and symbols are those that appear in the environment but without formal sanctioning. On a campus, these

Photo A11 Lost Sign

Photo A12 Redundant Signs

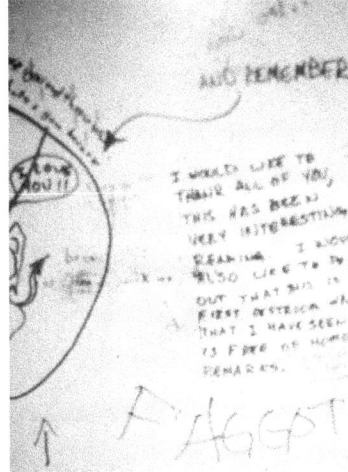

Photo A13 Graffiti

usually take the form of written signs that often give directions to a particular building or office (Photo A11). When these signs begin to appear in multiple numbers (redundancy), it is usually an indication that the physical environment is not giving sufficient way-finding cues (Photo A12).

Illegitimate signs or messages often take the form of graffiti. Most observers of the campus environment are quite familiar with campus graffiti. It can signal creativity and local issues or give insight into prevailing attitudes on complex issues such as tolerance of diversity (Photo A13). In addition, the failure to remove illegitimate and offensive graffiti also sends messages regarding the institution's values.

Summary

The concept of behavioral traces can be a useful tool for understanding organizations by observing the material culture. The environment is a medium of communication (Rapoport, 1982; Zeisel, 1975). Understanding this communication can assist in the campus appraisal and assessment process regarding campus issues, for example, diversity.

References

Banning, J. H. (1988). Behavioral traces: A concept for campus ecologist. *The Campus Ecologist, 7*(2), 1-2.

Banning, J. H., & McKelfresh, D. A. (1998). Using photographs of the housing mission Statementin staff training. *Talking Stick, 15*(8), 22-14.

Bechtel, R., & Zeisel, J. (1987). Observation: The world under a glass. In R. Bechtel, R. Marans, & W. Michelson (Eds.). *Methods in Environment and Behavioral Research* (pp. 11-40). New York: Van Nostrand Reinhold Company.

Bell, P., Fisher, J., Baum, A., & Greene, T. (1990). *Environmental psychology.* Fort Worth, TX: Holt, Rinehart and Winston, Inc.

Deasy, C. M. & Lasswell, T. (1985) *Designing places for people.* New York: Watson-Guptill Publications.

Porteus, J. (1977). *Environment and behavior.* Reading, MA: Addison-Wesley.

Rapoport, A. (1982). *The meaning of the built environment: A non-verbal communications approach.* Beverly Hills, CA: Sage Publications.

Steele, F. I. (1973). *Physical settings and organizational development.* Reading, MA: Addison-Wesley Publishing Company.

Weinstein, C., & David, T. (1987). *Spaces for children.* New York: Plenum Press.

Wohlwill, J., & Heft, H. (1989). The physical environment and the development of the child. In D. Stokols & I. Altman (Eds.), *Handbook of Environmental psychology, Vol. 1* (pp. 175-204). New York: John Wiley & Sons.

Zeisel, J. (1975). *Sociology and architectural design.* New York: Russell Sage Foundation.

Zeisel, J. (1981). *Inquiry by design.* Monterey, CA: Brooks/Cole.

ABOUT THE AUTHOR

James H. Banning

Jim Banning is professor emeritus in the School of Education at Colorado State University. After receiving his PhD in clinical psychology from the University of Colorado-Boulder, his career has focused on student services administration, ecological/environmental psychology, and the application of environmental psychology to educational settings. He has particularly focused on the application of the ecological perspective and the development of the campus ecology model and has taught a course in campus ecology in the Student Affairs in Higher Education Program at Colorado State University for more than 30 years and continues to teach an online version. His consulting work has been with universities and K-12 schools regarding visual messages. Jim's administrative leadership experience has included Director of Counseling and Testing, University of Colorado, Vice Chancellor for Student Affairs, University of Missouri-Columbia, and Vice President for Student Affairs, Colorado State University. During his career, Jim has authored and co-authored several books, book chapters, and journal articles on the ecological perspective of student services, including the recent publications of *Designing for Learning: Creating Campus Environments for Student Success, Student Affairs Leadership: Defining the Role Through an Ecological Framework, Campus Ecology and University Affairs: History, Applications, and Future,* and *Organizations at the Intersections of Place.*